THE BRUNCH TABLE

RECIPES, MENUS, & GAMEPLANS TO COOK, SHARE, & CREATE MEMORIES

Dimitra Khan

Edited by: Jessica Fateh & Malcolm Lewis

INTRO

The Table

In Greek, table: pronounced: trah-PEH-zee, is much more than just a piece of furniture. It's another word for meal. Honoring people with a meal is the way Greeks show their love. Is there even a better way?

Growing up, anytime my mom was having a "trahpezee", we knew that we would be eating our favorite foods together with friends and family. My fondest childhood memories are all woven together by the fabric of food, friends, family, and laughter, always in a laid-back setting. My summers spent in Greece, are filled with these memories. All of my relatives got together, either at my grandparent's village home or at one of my aunt/uncle's homes, almost every evening, ate delicious meals, outdoors, on tables (all kinds: wooden, folding, and plastic) joined together and covered with vinyl table cloths. All of the plates, glasses, and silverware in my grandma's cupboard came out. An eclectic collection. A little bit of everything. No fussing about matching anything. At the end of the meal, everyone got together, cleaned up, washed the dishes, then sat down to talk a little more. The kids ran around, played, and just had the time of our lives. These experiences filled me with a deep love of cooking and appreciation of sharing good food with friends and family. So, naturally, we opened a restaurant 10 years ago, I started a YouTube channel teaching cooking, and now I'm sharing my recipes with you in this book.

Brunch

It's no secret, breakfast is my favorite meal of the day. It's the only meal that dessert can be served as a main course: pancakes, French toast, and even yogurt parfaits can be pretty decadent. I love all of it. The egg and cheese dishes, the sides, it's comfort food in all of its glory. We sere breakfast all day at our café and have learned that it's a favorite for most people, too. We're all off on Sundays so our weekly family brunch usually begins at around 12 p.m. and sometimes lasts until 2pm, leaving everyone full until dinner time. My husband and I begin with hot tea and raisin bread smeared with butter and honey. The children usually eat bagel or any bread that may be leftover (banana bread, brioche, or something like that) while I'm fueling up for the day. Then, we have some sort of egg dish along with leftovers from the night before. Every now and then, I'll whip up a batch of French toast or pancakes. It's the most relaxed day of the week and we enjoy every minute of it together.

If you're new at entertaining, hosting a Brunch at home is the best way to get started. It's usually laid back, inexpensive, and most of the dishes served can be made ahead or in very little time. The menu can be as simple as putting together an oatmeal bar, preparing some deviled eggs, and serving some banana bread with tea or coffee. It can also be an elegant and fun way to celebrate a special day such as a baby shower, birthday, or Mother's Day. Guests arrive between Breakfast and Lunch, anywhere between 10 a.m. and 1 p.m. All the food can be served buffet style and you can enjoy the party as much as your guests will. I've learned that the most successful party/get togethers are the kind where the host spends the most time with their guests. If the menu is complex with the fanciest dishes that require too many ingredients and last-minute prep work, you will be slaving away in the kitchen away from your guests. I've learned this the hard way. So, in this book, I'll share my tried and tested foolproof recipes and menus so that doesn't happen to you. After all, the best way to show your love for the people that matter most is to have them over and share a meal together. These are the memories that will last forever.

I've been thinking about writing a cookbook for quite some time now. Sharing my recipes and YouTube tutorials while running our family restaurant, has given me a treasure trove of tips and tricks that I've wanted to put into print. I'm a normal, everyday mom of 5 that has a passion for showing my love through food and teaching you how to cook and share meals that will delight the people you care for.

For five years, I have been running a YouTube channel (sharing over 300 videos) that does just this. In this book, my recipes will be very easy to follow and loaded with make ahead tips to help you simplify the process. Working in the restaurant world these past ten years, I've learned a lot:
Many recipes (or parts of them) can be made ahead
Dressings can be made ahead and stored for a few hours and some recipes a few days
One simple recipe can be turned into countless dishes
Many dishes taste better if they're made ahead so that the flavors marry
Homemade food makes for the best gifts
Season every step of the way
Organization and prepare the secret to stress free entertaining.

I own and run a restaurant but have to truthfully say, hosting brunch at home beats going out to a restaurant, waiting in long lines to be seated, just to get your hot beverage served in a cold cup, hearing "I'm starving!" every 5 seconds, and paying a lot of money for eggs... I like to keep the menu simple while paying close attention to the details. The secret to stress free entertaining lies in the planning. Creating a menu that has some dishes that can be made ahead, some things that can be store bought, and it is equally important that the dishes are prepared using separate work spaces and appliances. For example, if all of your dishes require oven time, or stovetop cooking, you will run out of time and space to prepare them. So, I like to have one recipe that is baked, one prepared on the stove top, and something that doesn't need any cooking. Yogurt bars are a perfect example of something on the menu that doesn't need cooking. They can also double as dessert. A bread station is an example of something store bought (unless you're making my cinnamon rolls or brioche) that can be set out with jams, jellies, and flavored butters. I love serving scones because they can be made two weeks ahead of time and take less than 30 minutes to bake in the oven. Minimal effort, maximum flavor makes for successful entertaining.

Planning, Preparation, and Delight

In this book, I created 6 menus and have equipped you with well thought out "game plans" to make your entertaining stress-free.

I'm a huge fan of the buffet style set up. That way I can join my guests and eat together without all the fuss. You will notice a pattern in the menus and game plans associated with those menus. The food can all be served together meaning that it can all be set out at the same time. I've also learned that the secret to a successful party (get together) is prep and organization. Prepping a little bit a few days (and in some cases (weeks) before the party will ensure that you (the host/hostess) get to enjoy the day as much as your guests. If you are a very confident cook, feel free to adjust the game plan/menu to suit your entertaining style. One example can be to bake the scones (if serving) while your guests are eating their main course (instead of baking them as guests are arriving). They take less than 30 minutes to bake and that way, they can be served in all their flaky, buttery glory after the meal with coffee or tea. Part of every game plan is to clean your home the day before the party. I even include in each of the "day before" to-do lists, to set the table, and all the serving dishes, utensils, etc....The more you do before the day of the party, the more stress free your event (and you!) will be. You will also avoid headaches like scrambling and searching through every cabinet to find the serving platter for a particular dish or realize that the cord to the percolator is missing. It's happened to me more than once...

Create your own menus. I have included make ahead tips wherever it allows with each recipe. Even if you just make one recipe and buy everything else, it will be worth it. Accept help from your guests. Most of the time my guests offer to bring something. It doesn't have to be food. Ask them to bring flowers, just 1 stem each of an easy to find flower will help you with decorations. Combine the flowers into one bouquet or place 1-2 stems in glasses and set on the table. If you're assigning food to the guests, be specific to avoid duplicates. Food that doesn't need to be served hot is the most helpful: fruit salad, potato salad, dessert, etc.

Keep the menu simple; choose dishes (recipes) that complement each other and are easy to prepare. Everyone will enjoy the food and will be happy to spend time with you. Entertaining is not about showcasing our culinary skills or our impressive table settings and styles, but about creating memories by honoring the people we love, with our company and good food. I hope these recipes help you create the most beautiful memories!

CONTENTS

DRINKS

FRAPPE: GREEK STYLE ICED COFFEE •9

GREEK COFFEE•10

NUTELLA (CHOCOLATE HAZELNUT SPREAD) HOT

CHOCOLATE•12

SPARKLING MANGO & ORANGE REFRESHER•15

SPARKLING PINK GRAPEFRUIT MOCKTAIL•17

THE PERFECT CUP OF COFFEE•18

THE PERFECT CUP OF TEA•20

FRAPPE: GREEK STYLE ICED COFFEE

SERVES 1

Greek frappe is a drink made with Nescafe instant coffee that has a nice rich froth on top. It is the personification of summertime in Greece.

Shaker or hand blender
2 teaspoons Nescafe instant coffee
Sugar, optional (see Notes below)
1/3 cup water
Milk
Ice cubes
Optional: your favorite flavoring such as vanilla extract, pumpkin pie spice, hazelnut...

Notes on Adding Sugar to Frappe: There are 3 official ways to sweeten a frappe:
Sketos: translates to plain, which makes this unsweetened/no sugar
Metrios: translates to medium sweetness or 1 teaspoon of sugar
Glykos: translates to sweet, 2-3 teaspoons of sugar

Add instant coffee, sugar, and 2-3 tablespoons water to a shaker or the mixing cup of a handheld blender.

Shake or blend until a thick golden foam appears.

Fill a glass halfway with ice cubes and pour foam into it.

Pour the remaining water and fill with desired amount of milk.

Add flavoring at this point if using.

Place a straw in the glass and mix.

Serve immediately.

GREEK COFFEE

In Greece, coffee is a part of life. The day is started with a hot cup of this Greek coffee and enjoyed midafternoon while sitting with friends. The taste is rich and strong with a creamy froth on top whilst the grounds settle in the bottom of the cup. The sugar is cooked in the coffee and milk or creamer is never added.

Here is what you will need:
Coffee pot known as a briki
Greek coffee, my favorite brand is Loumidis
Demitasse cups/espresso cups
Sugar, optional
Water

Before you begin:
The coffee pot (briki, pronounced: bree-kee) is necessary to make the proper crema (foam) on top.

There are different briki sizes on the market, small ones for 1-2 cups and larger pots (holding at least 12 ounces) for larger quantities. Serious coffee drinkers own one of each. The larger pot is great for when hosting breakfast/brunch.

Be sure to use Greek Coffee, which is a finely ground blend of coffee beans.

The coffee is sweetened while it is cooking in the briki. Here are the 3 most common ways this is done:
Sketos: plain, unsweetened/no sugar
Metrios: medium sweetness; sweetened with 1 teaspoon sugar
Glykos: very sweet; sweetened with 2-3 teaspoons sugar
The demitasse cups are used as measures for the water

To make a cup of Greek coffee:
Measure 1 demitasse cup of water and place in the briki.

Add 1 heaping teaspoon of ground coffee and the desired amount of sugar. Mix well.

Place the pot over low heat and stir one last time.

When it begins to boil, lift the pot away from the heat using the handle.

When it settles down again place back onto the heat. This will help create a rich crema/foam on top.

Let it slowly come to a boil and rise to almost the top of the pot.

Remove from heat and pour into cup.

Serve immediately.

Notes: If making more than one cup in the same briki pot, follow the same instructions except when it's time to pour into the cups, pour a little in each cup and then go back to the first and pour until filled. This will distribute the grinds and the foam evenly.

NUTELLA (CHOCOLATE HAZELNUT SPREAD) HOT CHOCOLATE

This recipe is one of those that doesn't need a description. The title says everything needed to know about it. I'll just add three more words: decadent soul food.

¼ cup heavy whipping cream, or less for a lighter drink
¾ cup whole milk
1 tablespoon unsweetened cocoa pow-der
1 teaspoon confectioners' sugar
2-3 tablespoons chocolate hazelnut spread
A dollop of homemade whipped cream
Dusting of cinnamon

Place the milk, cream, sugar and cocoa powder in a small saucepan.

Mix it well and make it scalding hot.

Remove from heat and whisk in chocolate hazelnut spread until melted.

Pour in a cup and top with a dollop of homemade whipped cream.

Dust with cinnamon or cocoa powder and serve immediately.

SPARKLING MANGO & ORANGE REFRESHER

SERVES 8

Rich mango nectar combined freshly squeezed orange juice makes the most refreshing drink. The sparkling flavored water lightens this drink up and adds some fancy bubbly flair. Leave the water out when serving to children and just substitute some white grape juice instead.

1 and ½ cups freshly squeezed orange juice, chilled
1 and ½ cups mango nectar juice, chilled
1 (25 ounce) bottle orange or lemon flavored sparkling water, chilled
4-5 large strawberries, thinly sliced
A few sprigs of fresh mint

Mix the orange and mango juices in a pitcher.

Pour into a beautiful glass until halfway full.

Fill the glass with the sparkling water.

Garnish with strawberry slices and a sprig of mint.

Tips:
Add ice at the exact time of serving to prevent watering down the flavors of this drink.
To make it even more special, puree some berries with water to create flavored ice. This can also be done by freezing some orange juice to create orange flavored ice cubes.

SPARKLING PINK GRAPEFRUIT MOCKTAIL

What I love most about this drink is how pretty it is. Keep it simple by garnishing with a sprig of mint or rosemary. Make it extra special by topping with some organic rose petals or edible flowers. Beautiful, elegant, and refreshing.

2 cups freshly squeezed pink grapefruit juice, chilled
2 cups lime or lemon flavored sparkling water, chilled
Edible flowers or rose petals
A few sprigs of rosemary
Simple syrup: (note: you can leave out the simple syrup and use ginger ale or lemon soda instead)
1 cup water
1 cup granulated sugar
Optional: 1 teaspoon rose water

To make the simple syrup, combine the water with the sugar in a small saucepan. Keep stirring over medium heat until the sugar is completely dissolved.

Remove from heat and stir in the rose water, if using. Orange blossom water is a good substitute or leave it plain if desired. Set aside to cool. This syrup can also be stored in a glass mason jar in the refrigerator up to two weeks.

Fill the serving glasses halfway with the fresh grapefruit juice. Add 1 tablespoon of the simple syrup and stir.

Fill the glass with the sparkling water and stir to combine.

Garnish with a sprig of rosemary or with some edible flowers.

Note: If using edible flowers or rose petals, be sure that they are not sprayed with chemicals.

THE PERFECT CUP OF COFFEE

The magical formula for that perfect cup of coffee is pretty simple.

2 tablespoons ground coffee
6 ounces of water

Buy the best coffee beans that you can find. There are usually excellent coffee shops nearby that roast and grind their coffee. I highly recommend that you allow them to grind your coffee at the store with their burr grinder for your coffeemaker. It makes a huge difference.

Just as important as using high quality coffee is to use filtered water. Tap water is usually treated with chlorine and other chemicals that leave a strong taste in the coffee.

I don't own any fancy coffee makers other than a French press (which is my favorite way to prepare coffee) and an Italian espresso pot that heats on the stovetop.

Preparing coffee at home in a French press is simple.

Pull out the plunger.

Add 2 tablespoons ground coffee per 6 ounces water and stir.

Place the plunger back on top as to not loose heat, but don't press down yet.

Steep 3 and half to 4 minutes.

Press down on the plunger slowly. Pour and enjoy.

Always warm the cream and milk used to serve with coffee. I also always pour boiling water in the serving cups to keep them warm. There's nothing more awful than pouring steaming hot coffee into a cold cup.

BONUS: A super simple dessert is hot coffee with some ice cream scooped into it. It would be a great dessert/coffee bar addition.

THE PERFECT CUP OF TEA

Teatime is happy time. I love it so much that it must come twice a day. Everyday. Seriously. Some people start their day with coffee and the better half, with tea.... Joking... What I never joke about is bad tea. It's hard to ruin a cup of tea, yet unknowingly, its done too often. There's no reason for it. The convenience of choosing a tea bag that you love and pouring boiling water over it just can't be beat. No fussing with perfectly roasted beans, grinding with the proper equipment, to refrigerate or not, none of that. I mean, sure, you can buy loose tea and strain after it's steeped, but with all the excellent teabags on the market, you don't have to go through the trouble.

The recipe for the perfect cup of tea is quite simple:
1 English breakfast tea bag
6 ounces boiling water
Desired amount of hot cream or milk
Sugar or honey, to taste
A hot cup

To make the tea, bring water to a boil and simultaneously heat cream or milk to serve with the tea.

Spill the hot water that's in the cup warming it. Add 1 teabag to the empty cup.

Pour boiling water over the tea bag into the cup. Cover with a saucer and steep 4-5 minutes.

Remove teabag when the desired strength is reached.

Add the hot milk and sweetener if desired. Serve.

When making tea for a large crowd, I prefer to steep the tea in warmed up (same boiling water method) teapots.

Just add teabags to the pots and pour the boiling water inside. Cover, steep until desired strength is reached and serve.

If you've just recently developed a love for tea and want to share that love with friends, it might get difficult to warm up cups and may not have enough teapots. The perfect solution is to brew tea in a coffee percolator. This is my favorite way to serve tea at parties. Just keep in mind that since percolators keep passing hot water through the filler basket, the tea can get quite strong.

Here is how I make it:
I always make sure that the percolator is very clean, especially if I've used it to make coffee or any flavored tea.

Pour cold water into the percolator. 6-8 ounces (1 cup per person).

Insert the rod and basket along with the tea bags. 1 bag per cup.

Put the lid on and plug the percolator in and once the tea brew reaches your preferred strength, remove the tea bags from the basket and discard them.

Cover with the lid and the tea will remain perfectly hot until serving time.

Keep hot cream or milk nearby the machine along with sweetener and your guests can help themselves to a perfect cup of tea.

EGGS

BREAKFAST PIZZA•24

DEVILED EGGS•30

EGG & CHEESE BREAKFAST WRAP WITH ROASTED

POTATOES•32

GREEK STYLE SHAKSHUKA: EGGS POACHED IN A

SPICED TOMATO SAUCE WITH FETA•34

PERFECTLY POACHED EGGS•36

ROASTED BELL PEPPERS STUFFED WITH

SCRAMBLED EGGS•38

SCRAMBLED EGGS WITH SPINACH & FETA IN A

CROISSANT SANDWICH•40

SPINACH & FETA STRATA•42

SPRING VEGETABLE FRITTATA•27

BREAKFAST PIZZA

SERVES 4-6

One of the easiest dishes to serve at Brunch is this breakfast pizza. Your friends and family will be pleasantly surprised and impressed. Use whatever toppings you love on this. Leftover chicken, sausage, or deli meat will do. Substitute any shredded cheese for the mozzarella. Goat cheese instead of feta is lovely. Have fun with it!

For the pizza dough:
1 cup lukewarm water
1 teaspoon dry active yeast
½ teaspoon granulated sugar
2 cups bread flour
1 tablespoon olive oil
1 teaspoon salt

The toppings:
1 and ½ cups shredded mozzarella cheese
½ cup crumbled feta cheese
Sautéed spinach leaves (wilted in olive oil)
¼ cup sliced pitted olives
4 large eggs
Salt and freshly ground pepper, to taste

Optional: crushed red pepper flakes, any meat topping (leftovers work perfectly)
Optional spread: homemade pesto sauce

For the Pan Roasted Tomatoes:
2 pints cherry or grape tomatoes
2 tablespoons olive oil
Salt and freshly ground pepper to taste
2-3 scallions, finely sliced

For the herb oil: 2 tablespoons olive oil, 1/2 teaspoon oregano, 1/4 teaspoon salt

Combine the water, sugar, and yeast in the bowl of a tabletop mixer fitted with the dough hook attachment. Wait about 10 minutes for the yeast to activate. It is activated when a foamy cloud forms on top.

Combine the flour and salt in a bowl and mix well.

Add the olive oil and flour mixture to the activated yeast mixture in the bowl.

Knead for 8-10 minutes.

Place the dough into a greased bowl. Cover and set aside to rise until doubled in volume.

This can take 1 and ½ to 2 hours.

Preheat oven to 500 °F, 260 °C with a pizza stone on the middle rack.

Combine the herb oil ingredients in a small bowl and set aside.

Roll out the dough to 10-12 inches in diameter on a lightly floured work surface.

Place the dough on a baking tray lined with parchment paper.

If using pesto sauce, spread over pizza dough.

Sprinkle with the mozzarella cheese.

Top with the sautéed spinach leaves.

Sprinkle the crumbled feta cheese, olives, and crushed red pepper flakes.

Brush the edges of the crust with the herb oil.

Place the baking tray in the oven and bake for 8 minutes.

While the pizza is baking, prepare the tomatoes.

Heat a cast iron skillet to medium high heat.

Add the olive oil and tomatoes.

Cook for about 2 minutes.

Sprinkle a little salt and pepper over them and move them around in the pan so that they cook evenly on all sides. They may get a little bit of a char. Don't worry. That adds flavor. Lower the heat if they begin to burn.

Cook the tomatoes just until they release some juices and get a little wrinkly. Do not over-cook or they will melt. They should keep their shape and just get nice and juicy.

Remove from heat and top with the sliced scallions.

Take the pizza out of the oven and crack the eggs over the melted cheese and toppings.

Bake in the oven 5-10 minutes or until the eggs are cooked the way you like them.

Serve immediately with the pan roasted tomatoes.

Tip: For a crisp pizza bottom crust, after cracking the eggs onto the pizza, remove it from the baking tray and bake directly on the pizza stone. This will create a pizzeria type crust.

SPRING VEGETABLE FRITTATA

SERVES 6-8

A wonderful way to use leftover vegetables is to make a frittata with them. This is a basic recipe utilizing some of my favorite spring veggies, but you can make this today with whatever is in your refrigerator or freezer. Frozen peas, baby spinach, caramelized onions, and maybe some leftover roasted chicken makes for a delicious frittata. I just love the combination of zucchini and potatoes. Asparagus is one of my favorite springtime vegetables, so I use it as often as I can when it's in season. And, I always have a jar of roasted red peppers in my refrigerator ready to be added to just about anything. Altogether, it's a match made in heaven. Perfect for Brunch, lunch, or dinner.

1-pound potatoes, peeled and sliced 1/2 inch thick
3 tablespoons olive oil, salt and pepper to taste
¼ cup – 1/3 cup olive oil
Salt and black pepper to season vegetables
8 ounces asparagus, trimmed and cut ¼ inch pieces
1-2 zucchinis, sliced ¼ to ½ inch thick
1 roasted red pepper, canned or jarred, chopped
3 scallions, sliced
12 large eggs
¼ cup half and half
½ teaspoon – 1 teaspoon salt
¼ teaspoon black pepper
Pinch crushed red pepper flakes
4 ounces feta cheese, cubed or crumbled into chunky pieces
2-3 ounces shredded gruyere, cheddar, or gouda cheese

Preheat oven 350 °F, 177 °C.

Place the potato slices onto a baking pan, drizzle 3 tablespoons olive oil over top. Season with salt and black pepper. Bake until golden brown and cooked, 15 to 20 minutes.

Set aside to cool.

Add the asparagus to a 10-inch broiler safe skillet along with 2 tablespoons olive oil.

Season with salt and black pepper.

Cook over medium-high heat for about 3-4 minutes or until golden brown.

Add the zucchini slices to the pan and season with salt and pepper.

Add 1-2 tablespoons olive oil if necessary and cook over high heat 2-3 minutes until golden.

Add the scallions to the pan during the last minute of cooking asparagus and zucchini.

Remove from heat and mix in the chopped roasted red pepper and the cooked potatoes.

Taste and adjust seasoning if needed.

Whisk eggs, feta cheese, half and half, ½ teaspoon salt, ¼ teaspoon black pepper, and

crushed red pepper flakes in a large bowl until well combined.

Pour the egg mixture over the vegetables in the pan. Stir to combine using a wooden spoon or spatula.

Cook over medium heat 2- 3 minutes without stirring.

Transfer the pan to the oven in the middle rack and bake 15 minutes, or until just set.

Top with the shredded gruyere cheese, then broil 1-2 minutes or until the cheese melts and develops some color.

Allow to rest 5-10 minutes and serve warm.

Make Ahead Tip: The vegetables can be prepared the day before serving. Just warm them through in the pan before adding the eggs.

DEVILED EGGS

This classic old-fashioned appetizer is always a party favorite. It's a go to recipe when hosting brunch. I've noticed that even a basic, no frills deviled egg recipe disappears just as fast as the fancy stuff. They're simple and very economical to make when serving a crowd. Take this basic recipe and add your special twist to create countless variations.

6 large eggs
2 tablespoons mayonnaise
2 tablespoons Greek yogurt
1 teaspoon Dijon mustard
2 scallions, finely sliced
Salt and freshly ground pepper, to taste
10 Kalamata olives

Perfectly boiled eggs are a must for this recipe. Following these easy instructions for hard boiled eggs, will ensure beautiful golden yolks. No green ring around the yolks ever again. They will be easy to peel and picture perfect!

Place the eggs in a pot and cover with cold water. Make sure that the water is covering them at least 1 inch over top.

Bring to a boil. Turn off the heat and cover with the pot's lid. Let stand for 15 minutes undisturbed.

Carefully drain the eggs and fill the pot to cover them with cold water. Drain this water and cover with cold water one more time. Set aside to cool completely.

Peel the eggs. Using a knife and a damp towel, slice each egg in half lengthwise. Wipe the knife clean each time. Carefully remove the yolks and transfer into a mixing bowl.

Place the whites on a plate. Cover them with plastic wrap and set in the refrigerator while the filling is prepared.

Mash the yolks and add the mayonnaise, yogurt, mustard, salt and pepper. Mash together until creamy then pass them through a strainer.

Mix in the sliced scallions.

Remove the egg whites from the refrigerator and spoon or pipe the filling into the egg white cavity.

Arrange the eggs on a plate with olives in between.

Refrigerate until it's time to serve, covered loosely with plastic wrap or in an airtight container in a single layer.

Optional filling or garnish ingredients:
1 tablespoon finely chopped sundried tomatoes, packed in oil
Crumbled feta cheese (filling or garnish)
Finely chopped tomatoes (garnish)
Salmon roe (garnish)
Smoked salmon (either finely chopped for filling or rolled as garnish)
Sliced pickles as garnish, finely chopped pickles as filling ingredient
Sprigs of dill as garnish
Smoked paprika as garnish
Toasted sesame seeds as garnish

EGG & CHEESE BREAKFAST WRAP WITH ROASTED POTATOES

This recipe makes 2 small wraps or 1 big one. It depends on the size of the tortilla. The potato recipe feeds about 4-5 people. In my home however, 2 can finish the tray as soon as it comes out of the oven...

For the Roasted Potatoes:
6 medium Russet potatoes, peeled and cubed
1/4 cup olive oil
1 teaspoon salt
1 teaspoon oregano
black pepper, to taste
1/4 teaspoon crushed red pepper flakes
finely chopped scallions for garnish

For the Wrap:
2 large eggs
salt and pepper, to taste
1/2 avocado, sliced
1 tablespoon salsa
1 tablespoon sour cream
2 slices cheddar cheese
2 medium sized tortillas or 1 large

Preheat oven to 450 °F, 230 °C.

Place chopped potatoes on a baking tray. Drizzle with olive oil. Season with salt, peppers and oregano and mix well to coat. Spread the potatoes on the tray and bake for 20-25 minutes or until fully cooked.

Beat the eggs, salt and pepper with a whisk until fluffy.

Over medium heat, grease a frying pan with butter, generously. Pour egg mixture in the pan and cook the omelet.

Place the omelet on a plate and put the slices of cheese on top. Fold over so the cheese melts.
Warm the tortillas in the pan slightly.

Cut the omelet into two pieces if making 2 wraps.

Place one half of the omelet in the center of a warm tortilla. Put 3 slices of avocado, 1 dollop of sour cream and some salsa over the omelet. Roll the tortilla up and repeat the same steps with the second tortilla.

Serve with the potatoes on the side. Garnish the potatoes with some finely chopped scallions.

GREEK STYLE SHAKSHUKA: EGGS POACHED IN A SPICED TOMATO SAUCE WITH FETA

SERVES 4-6

Shakshuka, a popular North African dish consisting of eggs poached in a rich tomato sauce is a delicious dish that comes together in one pan. In 30 minutes! The sweet roasted red peppers, sliced olives and creamy feta cheese lend so much flavor that makes this a meal that can be enjoyed any time of day. I love serving it at brunch along with some tasted hearty bread and a salad.

¼ cup olive oil
1 small onion, finely chopped
1 roasted red pepper, diced
1 (28 ounce) can tomatoes, pureed
4-6 ounces feta cheese, crumbled
Salt & freshly ground black pepper to taste
½ - 1 teaspoon granulated sugar or honey
¼ teaspoon crushed red pepper flakes
1/4 teaspoon dried crushed oregano
7-8 Kalamata olives, pitted and sliced 6 large eggs
¼ cup fresh chopped parsley

Combine the olive oil with the onions in a large skillet over medium heat.

Cook until soft and golden. About 15 minutes.

Puree the canned tomatoes leaving them slightly chunky (or to your desired consistency).

Add the pureed tomatoes to the pan.

Season with salt, black pepper, oregano, and crushed red pepper flakes.

Taste sauce and add sugar if desired. Sometimes canned tomatoes can be acidic and adding a tiny bit of sugar or honey balances the flavors.

Cook over medium-high heat about 10 minutes or until the sauce has reduced and thickened.

Stir in crumbled feta cheese, sliced olives, and diced red peppers.

Make 6 indentations in the sauce and very carefully crack an egg into each space.

Season with salt and pepper.

Reduce the heat to low and cover the pan with a lid. Cook until the egg whites are set. About 10-12 minutes.

Sprinkle with chopped parsley and serve with warm pita or toasted homemade bread

PERFECTLY POACHED EGGS

MAKES 2 EGGS

Making poached eggs is much easier than one would imagine. They take any ordinary meal and turn it to a luxurious treat any time of the day, not just breakfast or brunch. The most important part of this recipe is to use the freshest eggs that you can find. Farm fresh would be ideal. The fresher the egg, the tighter the egg white. Meaning that it won't spread and create a mess in the pot. It's as simple as that. Serve poached eggs atop roasted vegetables, over toast with greens, in any sandwich, over stewed veggies, or in a salad.

2 cold fresh eggs
2 teaspoons white vinegar

Fill a saucepan with about 2 inches of water and bring to a simmer.

Crack the eggs into 2 ramekins or small bowls.

Pour the vinegar into the simmering water.

Using a spoon, stir the water to create a whirlpool.

Carefully drop one egg at a time into the center of the whirlpool.

Cook for 3-4 minutes or until the egg white is set. At around 3 and ½ minutes the white should be set and the yolk will still be runny. This all depends on the size of the egg. Keep an eye on it and don't check the egg before the 3-minute mark.

Lift the eggs out with a slotted spoon and drain on a kitchen towel.
Serve immediately.

Tip: If you are making poached eggs for a crowd, they can be made ahead and placed in ice water. When ready to serve, reheat them in warm water, drain, and serve.

ROASTED BELL PEPPERS STUFFED WITH SCRAMBLED EGGS

SERVES 2

A healthy and elegant way to serve up some scrambled eggs. Make this for 2 or 22.

2 bell peppers
Olive oil
Salt
4-5 eggs
2 tablespoons unsalted butter
½ cup -1 cup shredded mozzarella cheese
½ cup crumbled feta cheese
4 Kalamata olives, sliced
Salt and pepper
Dried oregano

Tzatziki Sauce for serving

Preheat oven to 400 °F, 200 °C.

Carefully slice tops of peppers off and set aside. Discard seeds and rinse and dry the peppers. Brush with olive oil and season with salt. Slice the tips of the bottom of the peppers off so that they are able to stand up without tipping over.

Place on baking pan and roast about 20 minutes or until softened and get some nice char marks. You can put them under the broiler the last 2 minutes.

Do not overcook them or they will fall apart.

Prepare the scrambled eggs by combining the eggs in a bowl with salt, pepper, feta cheese and oregano. Whisk the mixture together with a fork.

Roughly chop the spinach. Melt the butter in a large frying pan over medium heat. Add spinach and cook until wilted.

Add egg and cheese mixture and cook over medium-low heat constantly stirring with a spatula. Do not overcook the eggs.

Add mozzarella cheese and sliced olives and mix well.

Stuff the bell peppers with the scrambled egg and cheese mixture and serve immediately with some toasted bread or with roasted potatoes and tzatziki sauce.

SCRAMBLED EGGS WITH SPINACH & FETA IN A CROISSANT SANDWICH

Serves 2

One of the most popular sandwiches at our café. Once you taste it, you'll understand why this is the case. Toasting the croissant then filling it with the cheesy scrambled eggs creates a combination that cannot get more perfect. Unless, of course, it's dipped in tzatziki sauce.

2 croissants
4 large eggs
1-2 tablespoons unsalted butter
A handful of baby spinach leaves
¼ cup crumbled feta cheese
¼ cup shredded mozzarella cheese
Salt and freshly ground black pepper, to taste
1/2 teaspoon dried oregano or basil
2 tablespoons heavy whipping cream or whole milk

Preheat oven to 350 °F, 177 °C.

Combine the eggs, cream, salt, pepper, and feta cheese in a bowl and whisk together until well combined.

Slice croissants in half to separate the top and bottom. Place onto a baking sheet lined with parchment paper. Bake in the oven 3-5 minutes or until toasted.

Roughly chop the spinach leaves.

Heat butter over low heat in a pan until it melts.

Add chopped spinach to the pan and sauté for 2 minutes or until wilted.

Add the egg mixture to the pan and stir with a spatula or wooden spoon until curds form and almost cooked.

Sprinkle the shredded mozzarella cheese on top and stir to incorporate over low heat until cheese begins to melt.

Top with oregano and spoon into toasted croissants. Cut in half and serve immediately.

Tzatziki sauce goes great with this sandwich.

SPINACH & FETA STRATA

SERVES 12

This savory bread pudding is perfect for a family style brunch. A vegetarian main course that is hearty and flavorful. Guaranteed to impress!

1 (1 pound) loaf of bread, cubed
¼ cup olive oil
1 red onion, finely chopped
1-pound fresh baby spinach leaves
12 ounces feta cheese, crumbled
6 ounces gruyere or kefalotyri cheese, shredded
10 large eggs
1 cup whole milk
½ cup heavy whipping cream
2 teaspoons dried oregano
Salt and freshly ground pepper, to taste
¼ teaspoon crushed red chili flakes
1 roasted red bell pepper (from a jar or fresh), diced

Optional add ins: sliced mushrooms, drained (jarred) artichokes, sliced olives

Garnish: finely chopped chives or 2 scallions, finely sliced

Note: Any loaf of bread can be used in this recipe. My personal favorites are sourdough or French bread. Day old bread is best, but if you are using fresh bread it would be best to toast it in the oven so that it can absorb the custard easily.

Preheat oven to 325 °F, 160 °C.

Place the bread cubes on a baking tray and bake until golden all around. About 10 minutes.

Set aside to cool completely.

In a mixing bowl, combine the milk, cream, eggs, oregano, salt, pepper, and chili flakes. Whisk well to combine all the ingredients.

Cook the onions with the olive oil over medium low heat until soft and golden. About 10-15 minutes.

Add the spinach along with some salt and pepper. Cook 2-3 minutes until the spinach wilts.

Set aside and allow to cool.Add the cooled spinach and onion mixture to the egg custard along with the feta cheese and mix well.

Mix in the bread. Fold in the chopped bell peppers.

Pour the mixture into a 9 by 13-inch baking dish.

Cover with foil and place in the fridge overnight or at least 4 hours.

Preheat oven to 350 °F, 180 °Celsius.

Remove foil and place the tray in the center rack of the oven.

Bake 50 minutes.

Sprinkle the shredded cheese all over the top and bake 10 more minutes or until a toothpick inserted in the center comes out clean. The custard should be cooked.

Garnish with sliced scallions or chives. Cut into 12 equal pieces and serve.

This pairs well with tzatziki sauce and a tomato salad.

BREADS

CLASSIC FLUFFY PANCAKES

I must admit that we never eat pancakes for breakfast in our home. It's more like an after-breakfast treat. I would classify it as a dessert, but who's asking for clarification? Not me! These are super easy to prepare and disappear in no time.

1 and ½ cups all-purpose flour
3 teaspoons baking powder
½ teaspoon salt
1 and 1/3 cup whole milk
¼ cup yogurt
2 large eggs
3 tablespoons (1 and ½ ounces), butter, melted plus more for pan
2 teaspoons vanilla extract
2 tablespoons granulated sugar

In a large bowl, combine the eggs, milk, yogurt, sugar, and vanilla extract. Beat well to combine.

Combine the flour, salt, and baking powder in another bowl and whisk it all together.

Add the flour mixture to the egg mixture and mix until smooth.

Heat a greased cast iron pan or griddle over low heat.

Pour about ¼ cup of batter onto the pan for each pancake.

Once the pancake begins to bubble and the bottoms are golden brown, flip and cook 1-2 minutes more or until golden.

Stack the pancakes onto a plate and serve with maple syrup, honey, or a generous dusting of confectioner's sugar and fruit.

LEMON RICOTTA PANCAKES

MAKES 8-10 PANCAKES

Everyone has a basic pancake recipe, (there is one in this book in case you don't). Add these to your repertoire for special occasions. The ricotta cheese keeps these pancakes moist and fluffy. The refreshing lemon is just magical. They're perfect for an elegant Brunch, especially when served with this fresh blackberry sauce.

1 cup full fat ricotta cheese
¾ cup milk
¼ cup freshly squeezed lemon juice
2 tablespoons unsalted butter, melted plus more for greasing pan
½ teaspoon pure vanilla extract
1 cup all-purpose flour
1 teaspoons baking powder
½ teaspoon baking soda
¼ teaspoon salt
3 large eggs, separated
2 tablespoons sugar
1 tablespoon lemon zest

Blackberry Sauce:
12 ounces fresh blackberries
¼ cup granulated sugar
1 teaspoon cornstarch
1 tablespoon fresh lemon juice
3 tablespoons water

Begin by making the blackberry sauce. Combine all of the ingredients together in a saucepan and mix. Bring to a boil. Reduce heat to low and cook until sauce thickens slightly, and the berries break up.

Place the flour, baking powder, baking soda, and salt in a bowl and whisk to combine.

In a separate bowl, mix the ricotta cheese, milk, egg yolks, melted butter, lemon juice, and vanilla extract together.

Add the ricotta mixture to the flour mixture and mix until just combined.

Whip the egg whites on high speed until foamy.

Gradually add sugar and continue to whip until glossy and soft peaks form.

Take out 1/3 of the whipped egg whites and mix them into the batter. This will lighten the batter.

Gently fold in the remaining whipped egg whites into the batter using a rubber spatula.

Heat a cast iron pan or griddle over medium-low heat. Grease the pan with some butter.

Drop 1/3 cup of batter per pancake into the pan and spread into a 4-inch round.

Cook until the edges are set, and the bottom is golden brown. Flip and cook on the other side 2-3 minutes longer.

Stack the pancakes and dust with confectioner's sugar. serve immediately with the warm blackberry sauce.

Tip: If blackberries are not in season, feel free to use any fresh berries that you can find. Frozen berries are also a good substitute.

BASIC BRIOCHE DOUGH

I just love recipes like this one. Rich, buttery, and can be turned into so many different creations. Use it to make sweet or savory breads: hamburger buns, cinnamon rolls, sandwich loaf that can also be turned into a decadent French toast, fill it with shaved chocolate, fruit, nuts, the possibilities are endless.

1/3 cup lukewarm warm milk (approx. 100 degrees Fahrenheit)
1/4 cup sugar
1 tablespoon active dry yeast
3-4 cups all-purpose flour, divided
5 large eggs, room temperature
1 and 1/2 teaspoons vanilla extract (only needed if making a dessert version)
1 teaspoon salt
1/2-pound unsalted butter, softened
1 egg yolk and a little water

Combine the milk, sugar, yeast and 1 and 1/2 cup flour. Let it sit 30 minutes in the mixing bowl of a table top mixer, if you have one. This recipe is much easier to make with a mixer. It can be done by hand, but it will be sticky to work with. The mixture will form bubbles and a foamy cloud.

With the paddle attachment, beat in one egg at a time into the mixture and mix until smooth, about 3 minutes.

Add the vanilla extract if making a sweet bread.

Combine the remaining 1 and 1/2 cups flour with the salt and mix well.

Attach the dough hook to your mixer. Add the remaining flour mixture and knead for 10 minutes on medium speed.

While the mixer is still kneading the dough, add 1 tablespoon of softened butter at a time, allowing each piece to incorporate into the dough before the next addition.

Place the dough in an oiled or buttered bowl and cover with plastic wrap. Place in a warm place and allow to double in size. This should take anywhere between 1 to 2 hours, depending on the temperature in your home. (See tip that follows)

Allow to rise, brush with egg wash and bake until a toothpick inserted in the center comes out clean.

Once the dough rises it is ready. You may use it to bake your favorite recipe immediately, but it is much easier to work with after it is refrigerated for at least 3 hours or overnight. This dough is great sweet or savory.

Proofing tip: Run your dryer with a towel in it for 5 minutes. Place the dough on the towel, in the dryer. Make sure to keep the dryer turned off while dough is inside. Crack the door open a little to release some heat. The dough should rise to double its size in about 45 minutes. A great shortcut to use when in a hurry.

This dough is rich and delicious.

Use it to make one brioche loaf in a 9x5 inch loaf pan:

Grease the loaf pan and line with parchment paper. Form a log with the dough and place inside pan.

Cover with a kitchen towel and set aside to rise. About 1 and ½ hours.

Preheat oven to 400 degrees Fahrenheit, 204 degrees Celsius.

Brush the loaf with egg wash (1 egg yolk combined with 2 tablespoons milk or water)

Place in the center rack of the oven and reduce the heat to 350 degrees Fahrenheit, 176 Celsius and bake for 45-50 minutes or until a toothpick inserted in the center comes out clean.

Cool completely. Remove from pan and serve.

Tips: Create fancy textured bread by forming even ball shaped pieces of dough and then piling them in a loaf pan or Bundt pan.

TSOUREKI: GREEK STYLE BRIOCHE

MAKES 2 LOAVES

This traditional sweet bread is usually served at Easter. The mahlepi (the seed kernel extracted from cherry seeds) is what gives this bread its characteristic sweet aroma and delicious flavor, and worth the effort to find it. The best way to describe mahlepi's flavor would be a sweet combination of cherry with some almond in the background. Vanilla extract can be substituted, but to get that authentic tsoureki smell and flavor, get some mahlepi. Leftovers of this delicious brioche make the best French Toast.

For the starter:
1/2 cup milk, lukewarm
1 tablespoon active dry yeast
1 teaspoon sugar
2 tablespoons all-purpose flour

The dough:
4 cups bread flour
1 cup granulated sugar
3/4 cup lukewarm milk
2 large eggs
zest of an orange
1 tablespoon ground mahlepi
1/2 teaspoon salt
1/4 teaspoon ground mastic gum (optional)
2 ounces unsalted butter, softened at room temperature

egg wash: 1 egg yolk plus 2 tablespoons water

optional fillings: dried cranberries, raisins, chopped nuts, candied fruit, ground cardamom, vanilla or almond extract

Note: This dough can be prepared in a table top mixer or kneaded by hand in a large bowl or on the countertop. Using a mixer will require less kneading time. About 10 minutes. If making the dough by hand, knead it at least 15 minutes so that the gluten forms well to achieve the desired consistency and texture.

Combine the starter ingredients together in the bowl of a tabletop mixer.

Whisk and set aside for 10 minutes to activate the yeast. It is ready when a puffy cloud forms above the mixture.In another bowl, combine the flour, sugar, orange zest, salt, mahle-pi, and mastic gum together. Mix well to combine.

Once the yeast is activated, add all the remaining ingredients to the mixer's bowl. Turn the mixer on low and knead for 8 minutes.

Add the softened butter and increase the speed to medium and knead for 2 minutes.

Place some oil in the bottom of a large bowl and transfer the dough to the bowl. Toss around to coat and form a ball. Cover with plastic wrap and set aside in a warm place until doubled in volume. About 1 and 1/2 to 2 hours.

Punch down the dough to remove the air. Cut into 2 equal portions.

Cut each portion in thirds.

Roll each portion into about 13-inch-long ropes.

Form the 3 ropes into a braid and do the same with the remaining three ropes to shape 2 loaves of brioche.

Place both braided loaves onto a baking tray (18 by 13 inch) lined with parchment paper.

Cover with plastic wrap or with a clean towel.

Set aside until doubled in volume. If using the dryer trick, it takes about 45 minutes.

Preheat the oven to 350 °F, 180 °C.

Brush the tops of the brioche dough with the egg wash.

Optional: Place a hard boiled, dyed egg in the braids or top with sliced almonds.

Bake in the center rack of the oven for 30 minutes.

Remove from the oven and cool at least 30 minutes before serving.

Freezer Tip: Once baked and cooled, the bread can be frozen up to a month. Just make sure to wrap it well with plastic wrap.

Quick Rise Tip:
My favorite place to keep the dough so that it rises quickly is in the dryer. Here is what I do:

1) I put 3-4 clean bath towels in the dryer and turn it on (high heat setting) for about 5-6 minutes.

2) I place the bowl with the dough into the dryer (on top of the warm towels) and close the door.

3) Make sure the dryer is OFF!!

4) Remove from the dryer when it has doubled in volume.

This trick usually cuts 30 minutes from the rise time.

CHOCOLATE FILLED BRIOCHE

MAKES 1

1 recipe Brioche Dough

1 cup high quality chocolate chips, chopped
zest of an orange (optional)
Egg wash: whisk together 1 egg with 1 tablespoon
water

Orange Glaze:
1 cup confectioner's sugar
4 tablespoons orange juice

Chocolate Drizzle:
3 ounces chocolate (1/2 cup chocolate chips)
1/3 cup heavy whipping cream

Dust your work surface generously with flour. This is a sticky dough.

Roll out the dough into a large rectangle. Use a large cutting board or a 15x9 inch baking pan as a guide.

Zest an orange over the surface of the dough. Sprinkle the chopped chocolate all over the dough.

Beginning with the long end, roll it up tightly into a jelly roll shape.

Grease and dust your Bundt pan with flour. Place the filled dough into the pan and pinch both ends together.

Cover with plastic wrap and set aside to rise for about 30-45 minutes. The dough should come 3/4 way up the pan.

Preheat the oven to 400 °F, 200 °C.

Brush the top of the chocolate brioche dough with the egg wash and place in the oven. Im-

mediately reduce the temperature to 350 °F, 180 °C.

Bake for 40-45 minutes. A toothpick inserted in the center should come out clean.

Run a knife all around the pan to release the brioche.

Allow it to cool completely. Invert the brioche onto a cake platter.

Make the glaze by whisking the two ingredients together until smooth. Thicken it by adding more confectioners' sugar or thin it out by adding a little more juice.

Make the chocolate drizzle by pouring scalding hot heavy whipping cream over the chocolate and vanilla extract and mixing until smooth and glossy. Add more hot cream to thin it out if necessary.

Drizzle orange glaze and chocolate drizzle on top.

CINNAMON RAISIN BRIOCHE

This is so addictive that you will have to invite friends over to share it with just so that you don't end up eating it all by yourself!

1 recipe Basic Brioche Dough

1 and 1/2 cups raisins
1/4 cup dark brown sugar
1 cup cane sugar
ground cinnamon
zest of an orange (optional)

Egg wash: whisk together an egg with a tablespoon of water

Orange Glaze:
1/2 cup confectioners' sugar
1-2 teaspoons orange juice

Dust your work surface generously with flour. This is a sticky dough.

Roll out the dough into a large rectangle. Use a large cutting board or a 15x9 inch baking pan as a guide.

Combine both sugars, cinnamon, orange zest, and raisins in a bowl and mix well.

Sprinkle the mixture over the entire surface of the dough.

Beginning with the long end, roll it up tightly into a jelly roll shape.

Note: This can be baked in two 9x5 inch loaf pans or in a Bundt pan. In this recipe, the instructions will be for a Bundt pan which requires longer baking. If using the smaller loaf pans, cut the log in half and place each piece in the pans. Follow the remaining instructions and check it at the 35-minute mark.

Grease and dust your Bundt pan with flour. Place the filled dough into the pan and pinch both ends together.

Cover with plastic wrap and set aside to rise for about 30-45 minutes.

Preheat the oven to 400 °F, 200 °C.

Brush the top of the brioche dough with the egg wash and place in the oven. Immediately reduce the temperature to 350 °F, 180 °C.

Bake for 40-45 minutes. A toothpick inserted in the center should come out clean.
Run a knife all around the pan to release the brioche. Allow it to cool completely.

Invert the brioche onto a cake platter.

Make the glaze by whisking the two ingredients together until smooth. Thicken it by adding more confectioners' sugar or thin it out by adding a little more juice.

Cool completely and drizzle orange glaze on top.

HOMEMADE CINNAMON ROLLS

MAKES 12

Gooey homemade cinnamon rolls just can't be beat. They're perfectly soft, sweet, and fluffy. Definitely indulgent but worth every bite. They're great to serve for a holiday brunch when family may be visiting for out of town. Pop these in the oven and everyone will be ready at the table without the normal wakeup call. Make them extra special by adding some chopped peaches (when in season) or any other sweet fruit.

1 recipe homemade brioche dough

Filling:
4 ounces butter, softened at room temperature
1 and 1/2 cup brown sugar
1/2 cup granulated white sugar
2 tablespoons ground cinnamon
a pinch of salt
raisins, walnuts or pecans are an optional addition

Icing glaze:
4 ounces cream cheese, softened at room temperature
2 ounces unsalted butter, softened
2 cup confectioner's sugar, sifted
1 teaspoon pure vanilla extract
2-4 tablespoons milk or cream

On a floured surface, roll out the dough to a 15x9 inch rectangle.

Combine all of the filling ingredients well.

Spread the filling all over the surface of dough with your fingers or with an offset spatula.

Roll up the dough beginning at the long side. Pinch the edges to seal.

Cut into 12 equal slices.

Place the slices in a 9x13 inch baking pan and cover with plastic wrap. Set aside for 45 minutes till 1 hour until doubled in size.

Preheat oven to 375 °F, 190 °C.

Remove plastic wrap and place in oven. Reduce temperature immediately to 350 °F and bake for 30 minutes.

To make the icing, combine the butter with cream cheese and beat with a mixer or by hand with a fork.

Add the vanilla extract and the sugar a little bit at a time until well combined. Add the milk a tablespoon at a time until the icing is smooth and at a spreadable consistency.

As soon as the cinnamon rolls come out of the oven spread the icing all over them. Make sure to get the icing in the edges too.

Let them rest at least 45 minutes to set.

Serve with a nice hot cup of tea or coffee.

Enjoy!

TSOUREKI FRENCH TOAST

One of the best ways to take a basic recipe to the next level while keeping it very simple is to use very flavorful ingredients. Tsoureki, a Greek style brioche bread full of aromatic flavors such as mastic gum, vanilla, orange zest, and mahlepi creates an extraordinary French toast guaranteed to impress your guests.

6 slices tsoureki bread, 1 inch thick
3 large eggs
3 tablespoons sugar
1 cup whole milk
1/4 cup heavy whipping cream
ground cinnamon, to taste
1 teaspoon pure vanilla extract
2-3 tablespoons butter
Toppings: Greek honey, maple syrup, or confectioner's sugar and some fresh fruit

Combine the eggs and sugar in a 10 inch round deep-dish pie plate. Whisk well to break up the eggs and combine.

Add milk, cream, vanilla extract, and cinnamon. Whisk well.

Dip 3 slices of tsoureki into the custard. Pierce the slices with a fork so that the custard really soaks in.

Place a cast iron skillet over medium-low heat.

Melt a tablespoon of butter in the skillet and place the soaked tsoureki slices in the pan.

Cook about 2 minutes on each side until golden.

Repeat the same steps with the remaining 3 pieces of tsoureki.

Serve with fresh fruit and topped with maple syrup or Greek honey.

WHOLE WHEAT BANANA NUT BREAD

MAKES 2 LOAVES

This recipe is exceptionally moist with a lovely crunch on top from the walnuts. I made it using whole wheat flour for a nice healthy breakfast/brunch snack. You can absolutely make it with all-purpose white flour. It will be lighter as the whole wheat flour makes it denser. Whatever you choose to do, make it and enjoy with a nice hot cup of tea!

4-5 large, overripe bananas (I've used up to 6 banan-as; they make it extra moist)
2 large eggs
1/3 cup light olive oil
3 tablespoons plain yogurt
1 cup sugar
2 cups whole wheat flour
1 teaspoon baking soda
1/2 teaspoon vanilla extract
1/2 teaspoon salt
1/2 teaspoon cinnamon
1 cup walnuts or pecans

Preheat oven to 350 °F, 180 °C.

Grease two 3 x 7-inch loaf pans or a Bundt pan.

Beat the bananas with sugar to mash up nicely.

Add the oil, vanilla extract and yogurt and beat well. Add one egg at a time until combined.

Place all of the dry ingredients except for the nuts in a bowl and whisk them together.

Incorporate the dry ingredients in three batches mixing well between each addition. Do not over mix.

Divide the batter evenly into prepared pans. Sprinkle the nuts over the top.

Place the pan(s) on a baking sheet and put in the oven.

Immediately reduce the temperature to 325 °F, 160 °C and bake for 45 minutes to 1 hour, until the toothpick no longer has wet batter attached when checked.

Cool for 15 minutes.

Dust with some powdered sugar and enjoy!

Freezer Tip: This banana bread can be frozen after baked. Just remove from pan and wrap it nicely with plastic wrap.

SWEETS

HOMEMADE GRANOLA

MAKES 9 CUPS

I love breakfast. Everything about it. So naturally, I enjoy eating granola. Especially over Greek yogurt with honey or preserves. Anytime a meal can double as dessert, you just know it's going to be good! Take this basic recipe and substitute your favorite dried fruit and nuts to suit your fancy. Eat it for breakfast, serve at brunch, or give it as a gift in a nice mason jar.

3 cups rolled oats
1 cup sweetened shredded coconut
1 cup sliced raw almonds
1 cup cashews
¼ cup vegetable oil
½ cup maple syrup
¼ cup brown sugar
½ teaspoon ground cinnamon
½ teaspoon salt
1 teaspoon pure vanilla extract
½ cup dried cranberries
½ cup raisins

Preheat the oven to 300 °F, 150 °C.

In a large bowl, combine oats, coconut, and nuts. Stir to combine.

Combine the vegetable oil, maple syrup, sugar, vanilla extract, salt, and cinnamon. Whisk to combine.

Pour the syrup over the oat mixture and mix well with a spatula.

Spread the granola out onto a baking sheet.

Bake 45 minutes, stirring every 20 minutes so that they cook evenly.

Set aside to cool.

Mix in the cranberries and raisins and store in an airtight container.

ALMOND OR STRAWBERRY PALMIERS

MAKES 18-22 COOKIES

2 sheets puff pastry (8 ounces each), thawed
1/4 cup sliced almonds
sugar for topping

for the strawberry filling:
 1-2 cups strawberry jam

For the almond filling:
8 ounces almond paste
1/8 teaspoon salt
4 tablespoons unsalted butter, softened at room temperature
1/4 cup sugar
1/2 teaspoon pure almond extract
1 egg
zest of an orange

Preheat oven to 375 °F, 190 °C.

Make the almond filling by combining the almond paste, salt, and sugar in the bowl of a tabletop mixer. Beat until it breaks up and crumbles.

Add egg and almond extract. Beat until smooth.

Fold in the orange zest.

Roll out 1 sheet of puff pastry on a lightly floured work surface about 1 inch on all sides.

Spread half of the almond filling onto the pastry and sprinkle half of the sliced almonds over the filling.
Keep rolling the puff pastry toward the center until both sides meet.

Pinch the tops of both sides together and sprinkle with some sugar.

Slice the dough into 1-inch strips and place on a baking sheet lined with parchment paper.

Repeat the same process with the second sheet of puff pastry. You can slice this one as well into cookies or you can save it for later use by wrapping with plastic wrap and storing it in the freezer.

Strawberry Flavored:
Spread the jam across and roll both sides.

Bake for 35 minutes or until golden in the center rack of oven.

Remove from the oven and allow to cool.

Serve.

CLASSIC PALMIERS

MAKES ABOUT 20 COOKIES

I've never met a puff pastry recipe that I didn't absolutely love. These flaky, crisp, delicious French cookies are unbelievably easy to make, and they look and taste like you've spent forever making them. I always keep some puff pastry sheets in my freezer and make these cookies whenever friends stop by. Served alongside a nice hot cup of tea, they are perfection in every bite!

1 (8 ounce) sheet puff pastry, defrosted
3/4 cup sugar plus about ½ cup or more for the work surface
1/2 teaspoon cinnamon
1/8 teaspoon salt

Preheat oven to 400 °F, 200 °C

Mix the sugar, salt and cinnamon together in a bowl. Set aside. This will be used as the filling.

Spread some of the extra sugar on your counter/work surface and place the defrosted puff pastry over it.

Roll out the puff pastry so that it is about 1-2 inches wider on each side.

Evenly spread the sugar/cinnamon mixture all over the top of the puff pastry. Press it down with the rolling pin.

Roll the sides of the pastry (the long sides) towards the center until both sides meet and place on a baking sheet lined with parchment paper.

Chill for 15 minutes in the refrigerator so that they can firm up slightly. This will make them easy to slice.

Slice the dough into 1-inch strips and place on a baking sheet lined with parchment paper leaving some space in between each cookie.

Sprinkle more sugar mixture over the cookies if you like.

Bake for 15-20 minutes or until the sugar has caramelized and turned a beautiful golden brown.

Remove from the oven and allow to cool.

APPLE STRUDEL IN PHYLLO

SERVES 8

This gorgeous strudel has all of the comforting elements of fall. The house smells incredible while it's baking in the oven. Apple desserts, especially apples in some sort of flaky, buttery pastry, are a favorite in our house. We enjoy serving this all year long, not just around the fall and winter season when they're usually the most popular. It will become a favorite in yours too once you taste it. The crisp, flaky phyllo holds a warm, sweet apple pie filling that is the stuff that dreams are made of!

For the phyllo:
12 sheets phyllo pastry, thawed and at room temperature
8 tablespoons unsalted butter, melted
6-7 teaspoons granulated sugar

Apple filling:
5 apples (combination gala and granny smith) peeled, cored, and cubed
4 tablespoons unsalted butter
½ cup light brown sugar
¼ cup granulated sugar
3 heaping teaspoons corn starch
1 heaping teaspoon ground cinnamon
¼ teaspoon salt
1 teaspoon orange zest
½ cup dried cranberries
1/3 cup chopped pecans or walnuts

Preheat oven to 375 °F 190 °C.

Begin by making the apple filling. In a large, shallow saucepan melt butter and add apples. Add the brown sugar, white sugar, cornstarch, salt and cinnamon. Mix well and cook over high heat for a few minutes while constantly stirring to break up the sugar and combine all of the ingredients.

Once the apples release some juices and the sauce begins to thicken it is ready. Do not overcook or the apples will break down and become mushy. Keep in mind that they will continue to cook in the oven.

74

Remove from heat and add orange zest, cranberries and pecans. Mix well and set aside.

Line a sheet pan with some parchment paper. Place 1 phyllo sheet on the parchment paper and drizzle some melted butter over it. Sprinkle about 1 teaspoon or less of the granulated sugar. Repeat this process with the remaining 11 sheets of phyllo.

Arrange the apple filling in the center of the prepared filling (the long way) Brush the edges of phyllo with melted butter to create a seal.

Roll the phyllo over the filling carefully into a log. Keep the seam side down.

Brush with butter all around and bake for 30-35 minutes on the middle rack or until golden and crispy.

Allow to rest and cool for 15-20 minutes.

Dust with confectioner's sugar and cinnamon. Serve warm with some homemade whipped cream or with a scoop of your favorite ice cream.

BLUEBERRY & LEMON NOT JUST FOR COFFEE CAKE

SERVES 12

I'm not a real big coffee fan. I love my tea though.... That 15 minutes of peace and quiet. Just me, my tea and a nice pastry is like therapy. I look forward to it every day!! This cake goes perfect with tea and I originally wanted to call it "Blueberry Tea Cake", but I then thought about all the confusion that would cause: "is it cake made with blueberry tea? what is tea cake?" .... So, I opted out of being original and adventurous and kept things sort of basic. Everyone loves coffee cake, especially the yummy streusel topping! This cake is moist, light, flavorful and quick to put together. Substitute any berries: blackberries, chopped strawberries or mixed berries.

For the streusel topping:
2/3 cup of sugar
1/2 cup all-purpose flour
1/2 teaspoon cinnamon
1 stick (4 ounces) cold unsalted butter cut into cubes
a pinch of salt

For the batter:
1 and 2/3 cups all-purpose flour
1 teaspoon baking powder
1/2 teaspoon salt
1 and 1/2 sticks (6 ounces) unsalted butter, soft and at room temperature
3/4 cups sugar
2 large eggs
1/4 cup whole milk
1 and 1/2 teaspoons pure vanilla extract
zest of a lemon
3 cups (1 lb.) blueberries (dusted with flour)

Preheat the oven to 350 °F, 177 °C. Grease a 9 by 13-inch baking pan generously with butter.

In a large bowl, beat the butter and sugar together until fluffy and combined. Add the eggs, milk, lemon zest and vanilla extract. Beat until completely combined.

Sift the flour, baking powder and salt in a bowl.

Slowly add the sifted dry ingredients into the wet ingredients in 3 batches. Mix until just combined. Do not over mix otherwise your cake will not be light.

Dust about a teaspoon of flour over the blueberries and mix them gently with your fingers so that they get lightly coated with flour. This will help them stay suspended inthe cake and will prevent them from sinking to the bottom.

Fold the blueberries into your cake batter with a rubber spatula.

Spread the batter evenly into the prepared baking dish.

Now, make the streusel topping: In a bowl, whisk together the flour, sugar, salt and cinnamon. Sprinkle the cold butter on top. Using a fork or pastry cutter, cut the butter until the mixture becomes crumbly.

Sprinkle the topping over the cake.

Bake for 35-40 minutes or until a toothpick inserted in the center of the cake comes out clean and the top is golden.

Allow the cake to cool for about 15-20 minutes. Cut it into squares and serve.

To make Blueberry & Lemon Streusel Muffins:

Place 1/4 cup scoop of this batter in 17 cupcake tins lined with paper cups. Top with a heaping tablespoon of streusel and bake at 350 °F, 177 °C for 20 minutes or until a toothpick inserted in the center comes out clean.

Bake 1 tray at a time in the center rack of oven.

KARIDOPITA: WALNUT & HONEY CAKE

SERVES 12

Stick to the classics, "they" say, and you can't ever go wrong. "They" are right! This cake has all the flavors of traditional Greek desserts: cinnamon, a hint of cloves, orange, and honey syrup. The olive oil keeps it nice and light. However, my favorite thing about this recipe is that it can be made a few days ahead of time, in a simple 9 by 13-inch baking tray, cut into squares and served. Effortlessly! Of course, you can get fancy and make little cupcakes, bake in a decorative Bundt cake pan, etc.... but, keeping things simple means more fun with your guests.

The cake:
1 cup light olive oil
6 eggs
1 cup whole milk
1 cup sugar
2 cups all-purpose flour
4 teaspoons baking powder
1 teaspoon baking soda
2 teaspoons ground cinnamon
1/4 teaspoon ground cloves
1/4 teaspoon salt
1 and 1/2 cups coarsely ground walnuts plus 1 tablespoon flour

The Honey Syrup:
2 cups sugar
1 cup honey
3 cups water
1/4 teaspoon whole cloves
1 cinnamon stick

The garnish:
1/2 cup ground walnuts
1 teaspoon powdered sugar
a pinch of ground cloves
1/4 teaspoon ground cinnamon

Preheat the oven to 350 °F, 180 °C. Grease the bottom and sides of a 9 x 13-inch baking dish.

Beat the eggs and sugar together for a few minutes until thick and pale. Add the olive oil and milk.

Beat well to incorporate.

In another bowl, sift the flour, baking powder, baking soda, ground cinnamon, ground cloves and salt.

Slowly add them to the egg mixture while gently whisking just until incorporated and most of the batter is smooth. Do not over mix! Otherwise your cake will not be light and fluffy.

Combine the ground walnuts with the tablespoon of flour and mix it in a separate bowl.

Fold in the walnuts gently with a spatula.

Pour the batter in the already prepared baking dish.

Bake it for about 45 minutes or until a toothpick inserted into the center of the cake comes out clean.

While the cake is baking, prepare the honey syrup.

Combine all the ingredients into a saucepan.

Bring it to a boil while stirring. Let it continue to cook over medium heat for about 5 minutes until very slightly thickened.

Turn off the heat and allow the syrup to cool completely before removing the cloves and cinnamon stick.

As soon as the cake is done baking, remove it from the oven and poke it all over with a toothpick.

Pour all the cooled honey syrup over the cake slowly, allowing it to be absorbed.

Combine the walnuts with the powdered sugar, cinnamon and cloves and sprinkle over the cake to garnish.

*Tip: Begin by measuring out your dry ingredients so that you will have fewer things to clean. Also, measure your honey after measuring the oil for the cake. Doing this makes the honey slide out of the measuring cup much easier.

BLUEBERRY STRUDEL WITH A GREEK YOGURT SAUCE

MAKES 2 STRUDELS

This blueberry strudel is so delicious that you will be happy the recipe makes two. The second can be frozen before baking for 2-3 weeks. It has never lasted longer than a week in my freezer, but it will stay fresh for that long. Serve it at brunch with hot tea and coffee and enjoy every flaky bite.

1-pound phyllo pastry, thawed and at room temperature (you will only use 12 sheets)
1/2-pound butter, melted
about 12 tablespoons sugar

For the filling:
4 cups fresh blueberries
3/4 cup sugar
zest of half of a small lemon
5 tablespoons corn starch
2 tablespoons lemon juice (freshly squeezed)
1 tablespoon unsalted butter
pinch of salt (about 1/8 - 1/4 teaspoon)

Sauce:
1 cup Greek yogurt
1/4 cup powdered sugar
lemon zest

Preheat oven to 400 °F, 200°C.

Begin by making the blueberry filling: Place one cup of the blueberries in a small saucepan with the sugar, salt, lemon juice, lemon zest, butter and corn starch. Cook over medium heat until the juices release. Keep mixing and mashing the berries. This will create a beautiful, thick blueberry sauce. Remove from heat. Add the remaining 4 cups of blueberries to the sauce and mix well. Set aside.

Prepare the phyllo sheets. Keep two kitchen towels ready; a damp one and a dry one. Cover the phyllo pastry first with the dry towel and then with the damp towel. This will keep them from drying out and crumbling.

Place one sheet of phyllo on a baking sheet lined with parchment paper. Drizzle some melted butter on it and brush all over. Sprinkle about a tablespoon of sugar over the entire phyllo sheet and repeat this step with 5 more sheets.Brush melted butter around the border of the stacked phyllo sheets.

Place half of the blueberry filling in the center. Fold the phyllo over the filling like a letter (the wide side). Press the sides down.

Brush the top with more melted butter and sprinkle with sugar.
Repeat the same steps to form the second strudel.

Place in the center rack of your oven.
Reduce heat to 350 °F, 180 °C and bake for 35-40 minutes or until golden brown.
Allow to cool 15-20 minutes before serving.

Prepare the yogurt sauce by whisking the Greek yogurt and the sugar together until combined. Zest a lemon over the yogurt and serve!

Freezer tip: Store the extra unbaked strudel, tightly wrapped in plastic in the freezer. When ready to bake, unwrap, place on baking tray, brush with egg wash, and cover with foil. Bake 45 minutes covered, then uncover and bake 15 minutes or until golden.

BLUEBERRY TURNOVERS

MAKES 12

Flaky puff pastry filled with a homemade blueberry filling that can be made ahead, frozen and baked in 30 minutes. Serve it as is or with a scoop of ice cream for an impressive and delicious dessert. You can't beat that!

2 (8 ounces each) sheets of puff pastry, defrosted
3 cups fresh blueberries (separate into: 2 cups and 1 cup)
1/2 cup sugar
2 tablespoons corn starch
1 tablespoon butter
Zest of half a lemon
juice of half a small lemon
pinch of salt

Egg wash: 2 egg yolks beaten with two tablespoons of milk or water

confectioner's sugar for dusting

Preheat oven to 350 °F, 260 °C.

Combine 2 cups of the blueberries, butter, sugar, cornstarch, lemon zest, lemon juice and salt in a small saucepan. Cook over medium heat until juices are released, and the mixture thickens slightly. It will continue to thicken as it cools so be careful not to overcook.

Add the remaining one cup of fresh blueberries and mix well. Allow to cool.

Roll out each sheet of puff pastry into a 12-inch square.

Cut each sheet into 4 smaller squares, 6 inches each.

Place one and one-half tablespoons of blueberry filling in the center of each small square and brush the edges with egg wash.

Fold over to make a triangle, pressing the air out.Place each turnover on a parchment paper lined baking sheet leaving a few inches of space between them. They will puff up while baking.

Press the edges down with a fork to seal and create a decorative border.

Make a small slit on top of each turnover so that the steam can escape during baking.

Brush with egg wash.

Bake for 25-30 minutes or until puffy and golden brown on top.

Allow to cool and dust with confectioner's sugar.

Enjoy! They taste even better with a scoop of vanilla ice cream.

CHOCOLATE HAZELNUT BAKLAVA ROLLS

MAKES 10 ROLLS

Crisp, buttery layers of phyllo, filled with chocolate hazelnut spread and drizzled with an aromatic syrup. What could be better? I just love desserts like this one for so many reasons. The ingredients are few and easy to find, the taste is just so delicious, and they freeze well. So, they're perfect for serving when entertaining, especially since they can be made weeks ahead of time and then just popped in the oven the day of the party.
Did I mention that it takes less than 35 minutes to bake these decadent rolls?

1 cup chocolate hazelnut spread, homemade or store-bought
1/2 cup toasted chopped hazelnuts
5 sheets phyllo pastry
1/4-pound unsalted butter, melted
For the syrup:
1/2 cup sugar
1/4 cup water
juice of 1/2 orange
Optional: powdered sugar and cocoa powder
sliced bananas for serving

Preheat oven to 375 °F, 190 °C.

Begin by making the syrup.

Combine all the syrup ingredients into a small saucepan. Mix well and bring to a boil. Cook just until the sugar is dissolved.

Set aside to cool completely.

Cut the phyllo in half and stack covered with a slightly damp towel to prevent it from drying out.

Line a baking tray with parchment paper.

Brush a sheet of phyllo with melted butter. Place a tablespoonful of chocolate hazelnut spread and top with some chopped hazelnuts.

Fold the sides of the phyllo pastry over the filling and brush with some melted butter. Roll up and set on the baking pan.

Continue the same process.Brush the tops of all the rolls with the remaining melted butter. Pour any remaining butter on top.

Bake in the preheated oven 15-20 minutes or until golden all around.As soon as the baklava rolls come out of the oven, pour the syrup over them.

Let them soak in the syrup for 5 minutes then flip them over.

If you are not soaking these with syrup just dust them with confectioner's sugar and cocoa powder.

Serve warm over some banana slices.

Make Ahead Freezer Tips: Follow the instructions up until baking. Do not bake these before freezing. Butter them and cover with plastic wrap. Double wrap if necessary. Place in the freezer. When ready to bake, preheat the oven to 350 degrees Fahrenheit, 177 degrees Celsius, and bake about 30- 35 minutes or until golden.
Follow the remaining instructions and enjoy!

CHOCOLATE HAZELNUT PAVLOVA

SERVES 6-8

Pavlovas are simply gorgeous. This recipe is extra special with the addition of hazelnuts and cocoa. Perfectly crisp exterior and chewy interior. They look fancy but are incredibly easy to make and assemble. If hazelnuts are hard to come by feel free to substitute almonds.

For the meringue:
5 ounces hazelnuts
4 (extra-large) egg whites, at room temperature
a pinch of salt
1 cup sugar
2 teaspoons corn starch
2 tablespoons cocoa powder
1 teaspoon pure vanilla extract
1 teaspoon white wine vinegar

For the cream:
1 and 1/2 cups cold heavy whipping cream
½ cup confectioner's sugar
1 teaspoon pure vanilla extract

12 ounces fresh raspberries or assorted berries for garnish

Preheat oven to 300 °F, 150 °C.

Place the hazelnuts on a baking sheet and toast in the oven for 8 minutes.

Carefully place the toasted hazelnuts onto a kitchen towel and rub until most of the skins are released.

Allow to cool completely.

Pulse in a food processor until finely ground.

Line a baking sheet with parchment paper.

Draw an 8-inch circle on the parchment paper.

Turn the paper over so that you do not get pencil marks on your meringue.

Add the egg whites and salt to the bowl of a table top mixer fitted with the whisk attachment.

Whip them until frothy.

While the mixer is running, slowly add the sugar and vanilla extract until the mixture becomes stiff and glossy. About 6 minutes.

Sift the cornstarch and cocoa powder over the whipped egg whites.

Add the vinegar and carefully fold it in with a spatula along with the ground hazelnuts.

Spread the mixture onto the parchment paper inside the circle. Spread it carefully, creating a bowl shape in the center. Create swirls and spikes around the edges.

Bake for one hour.

Turn the oven off after one hour and leave the meringue inside for 1 more hour. It will be crispy on the outside and like a marshmallow on the inside.

Prepare the whipped cream while meringue is cooling. Combine the heavy whipping cream, vanilla, and sugar in a large bowl. Whip until thick and creamy.

Fill the center of the cooled meringue with whipped cream and top with the berries.

SHORTBREAD COOKIES

MAKES ABOUT 24 HEARTS

This recipe is a must have for any serious baker. At the bakery, we use it to make all different kinds of cookies: Linzer sandwich hearts, plain shortbread, specialty shaped cookies for party favors (tea bags, stars, you name it!), tart shells, pie crust, crumbles.... Create sweet, crisp, buttery cookies for all occasions using this basic recipe.

3/4-pound unsalted butter, softened at room temperature
1/2 cup granulated sugar
1/2 cup confectioner's sugar
1/2 teaspoon salt
2 teaspoons pure vanilla extract
3 cups all-purpose flour
confectioner's sugar for decorating
your favorite jam, preserves, curd, chocolate for filling the cookies

optional: melted white, semi-sweet, or dark chocolate for decorating or dipping, sprinkles, ground or sliced nuts for
decorating, jam, curd, chocolate, buttercream for filling

Combine the butter, salt, both sugars, and vanilla extract in the bowl of a table top mixer fitted with the paddle attachment.

Beat beginning on low speed until all of the sugar is incorporated. Increase the speed to high and beat until creamy. Scrape down the sides of the bowl at least once in between mixing so everything is evenly incorporated.

Add the flour in 2-3 batches mixing on low speed.

Beat until a dough ball begins to form.

Some crumbled dough may remain at the bottom of the bowl. This will all come together when it's rolled out on the counter.

Place the dough onto a clean work surface (counter) and press it together to form a disk. A ball can be formed first and then press it down with your palm to form the disc.

Lift the disk and sprinkle the work surface with some all-purpose flour.

Place the dough over it and sprinkle the top with a light dusting of flour along with the rolling pin. This will help the dough roll out easily.

Take care to not put too much flour or this will yield tough cookies.

Roll the dough out to a quarter inch in thickness for thinner cookies or up to half an inch for thicker cookies.

Thinner cookies are ideal when making linzer (sandwich style) cookies.

Cut the cookies out using your favorite cutter. Keep a bowl with some flour nearby in case the cookie cutter becomes sticky.

Place the cut-out cookies onto baking sheets lined with parchment paper leaving some room in between for baking.

Combine all the leftover dough together and roll out again.

If making the sandwich cookies, use a smaller cutter to cut out the centers of the cookies AFTER they are placed on the baking sheet. This will keep them from falling apart or breaking.

Chill the cookies in the freezer or refrigerator 15 -30 minutes so that they can retain their beautiful shape while baking.

Preheat the oven to 325 °F, 160 °C.

Bake the cookies 15- 20 minutes or until they are golden around the edges.

If baking more than one tray at a time, rotate the trays halfway through baking to ensure that both trays bake evenly. Do this by switching the bottom tray to the top and vice versa.

Cool completely.

Spread your favorite filling (jam, curd, chocolate, buttercream) over the top of the flat side (bottom) of cookie.

Dust the cookies with the cut-out center with powdered sugar.

Place the cut-out cookie over the filling.

There are so many variations that can be created with this simple recipe. It is completely up to you!

These cookies can be stored (before filling) in an airtight container at room temperature up to two weeks.

The uncooked cookie dough can be tightly wrapped in plastic wrap then placed in a freezer bag and can be stored in the freezer up to two months. Just completely thaw the frozen dough out, roll out and cut into your favorite shapes, then bake.

WHOLE WHEAT BLUEBERRY MUFFINS

MAKES 12

The Dry Ingredients:
2 and 1/4 cups whole wheat flour
1/2 teaspoon salt
1 teaspoon baking powder
1/2 teaspoon baking soda
1 teaspoon ground cinnamon

The Wet Ingredients:
1 cup sugar
1/3 cup vegetable oil
1 and 1/2 cups plain yogurt, or 3/4 cup Greek yogurt
with 3/4 cup milk)
1 teaspoon pure vanilla extract
1 egg
1 cup blueberries, fresh or frozen will do
zest of an orange or a lemon

Cinnamon sugar topping:
3 tablespoons sugar plus 1 tablespoon cinnamon

Preheat oven to 400 °F, 200 °C.

Combine all of the dry ingredients except for the citrus zest together and pass through a sifter. Add the zest and set aside.

Beat together the sugar, oil, and egg until combined.

Add the yogurt and vanilla extract and mix to combine.

Add the flour mixture in 3 batches and mix just until incorporated.

Carefully fold in the blueberries with a spatula.

Line a muffin tray with paper liners and scoop the batter in each cup 3/4 of the way full.

Sprinkle the cinnamon sugar over each muffin.

Bake in the center rack of your oven for 18-20 minutes or until a toothpick that is inserted in the center of a muffin comes out clean or with dry crumbs.

Serve with a nice hot cup of tea.

CINNAMON RAISIN & WALNUT SCONES

MAKES 8 SCONES

This recipe came about while recipe testing scones for a good friend's baby shower. The warmth from the cinnamon with the earthy and sweet tones coming from the raisins and walnuts was to die for. Pecans can easily be substituted for the walnuts and will still yield a lovely scone. My favorite accompaniment to these is a lovely apricot butter.

6 ounces unsalted butter, cold and diced

The Dry ingredients:
2 cups all-purpose flour (plus a little more for dusting your work surface)
1/4 cup granulated sugar (plus extra for sprinkling before baking)
1 tablespoon baking powder
1 rounded teaspoon cinnamon
1/2 teaspoon salt

The Wet Ingredients:
1/2 cup heavy whipping cream, cold
2 large eggs, cold
1 teaspoon vanilla extract

The Mix Ins:
1/2 cup raisins
1/2 cup chopped walnuts

Apricot Butter:
Beat 4 ounces softened, unsalted butter with 1/8 teaspoon salt and 2 -4 tablespoons apricot butter until fluffy.

Preheat the oven to 425 °F, 220 °C.

Combine the dry ingredients in the bowl of a table top mixer and mix to combine with the paddle attachment.

In another bowl, whisk together the wet ingredients.

Add the cold diced butter to the flour mixture and mix on low speed until it resembles coarse meal, taking care not to melt the butter.

Add the wet ingredients and mix until well combined (making sure not to over work the dough) until the dough comes together.

Add the walnuts and raisins and mix just until combined. Do not over mix. The dough will be sticky. Don't worry!

Lightly flour your counter or work surface and form the dough into a ball.

Roll the dough out into a circle or square about 1 inch in thickness.

Use your favorite cookie cutter and cut out the scones or cut like you would slice a pizza into 8 equal slices.

Place the scones on a baking sheet lined with parchment paper. Freeze for 15 minutes or until firm.

Sprinkle with sugar.

Bake for 20-22 minutes or until golden brown.

Allow to cool for 10-15 minutes.

Dust with confectioner's sugar and serve with apricot butter.

Freezer tip: Place unbaked scones on a pan and freeze until firm. Transfer to a freezer bag and store up to 3 weeks. When ready to bake, preheat the oven (same temp.) and follow the recipe instructions above.

CRANBERRY & LEMON SCONES

MAKES 8

What's better than a flaky, buttery scone? A lemon flavored one of course!
The lemon in these really complements the sweet chewy dried cranberries. Serve these
at brunch with a cup of tea and some Devonshire cream and transport your guests to
a British tea room. This is another one of those delicious recipes that freeze beautifully
(before baking). So, be sure to make a double batch if you can. Who doesn't enjoy having an
emergency stash of ready to bake scones.

6 ounces unsalted butter, cold and diced

The Dry Ingredients:
2 cups all-purpose flour (plus a little more for dusting
your work surface)
1/4 cup sugar
1 tablespoon baking powder
1/2 teaspoon salt
The Wet Ingredients:
1/2 cup heavy whipping cream, cold
2 large eggs, cold
1 teaspoon vanilla extract

The Mix Ins:
1 and 1/2 teaspoons lemon zest
1/2 cup cranberries (dried apricots are a great substitute)

For the egg wash:
1 egg with 2 tablespoons water whisked well

The glaze: 1/2 cup powdered sugar with about 2-3
tablespoons freshly squeezed lemon juice

Preheat the oven to 400 °F, 200 °C.

Combine the dry ingredients in the bowl of a tabletop mixer fitted with the paddle attachment. (If using a food processor, use the blade attachment). Mix well to combine.

Mix in the butter until the mixture resembles coarse meal.

In another bowl, whisk together the wet ingredients.Add this wet ingredients to the mixer and beat just until it comes together and forms a ball of dough.

Add the cranberries and mix until combined. Do not over mix. Pieces of butter should remain visible throughout the dough. Overmixing will cause the butter to melt and will produce hard scones.

Lightly flour your counter or work surface and place the dough on it.

Roll the dough out in a circle almost an inch thick and cut it into 8 triangles, just like pizza slices.

Place the scones on a baking sheet lined with parchment paper.

Brush with the egg wash.

Bake for 20-22 minutes or until golden brown.
Allow to cool for 10-15 minutes.

Dust with confectioner's sugar or with the lemon glaze.

Note: This recipe can be made without the use of any equipment other than a large bowl and your hands to break up the butter. However, if you own a food processor or a table top mixer, you can use either one of those helpful machines.

Freezer tips: same as cinnamon raisin & walnut scones

FETA & DILL SCONES

MAKES 16

Is it a scone? Is it a biscuit? Call it whatever you want. Just know that these little buttery confections are delicious! They're wonderful served as a side to salad or soup and elegant enough for high tea. You know how much I enjoy make ahead recipes that freeze well. These are perfect for the freezer so that you can bake just one for yourself or a batch for a party.

6 ounces cold unsalted butter, diced
The Dry Ingredients:
3 cups all-purpose flour, plus more for kneading
2 tablespoons baking powder
2 tablespoons dried dill
1 tablespoon sugar
1 teaspoon salt
1/4 teaspoon black pepper

The Wet Ingredients:
3 large cold eggs, beaten
1 cup Greek Yogurt, chilled

The Mix Ins:
1 cup diced feta cheese (I highly recommend a sheep's milk kind like "Dodonis")

For the Egg Wash:
1 egg beaten with 1 tablespoon milk or water,

Preheat the oven to 400 °F, 200 °C.

Combine all of the dry ingredients in the bowl of a stand mixer fitted with the paddle attachment. Mix to combine.

Add the diced butter and mix on low speed until the butter is coated with the dry ingredients and it becomes pea sized.

Whisk the wet ingredients and add to the mixer. Mix on low speed just until everything comes together. The dough will be very wet.

Fold in the feta cubes being careful not to mash them up too much.

Flour your work surface generously and place the dough on top of it.

Roll the dough 3/4 inch thick. Cut it into your favorite shape. I like cutting it with a square cookie/biscuit cutter. You can also form the dough into a rectangle or square and cut out the scones with a knife.

Place the scones on a baking sheet lined with parchment paper. Chill in the freezer for 15 minutes or until firm.

Brush the tops with egg wash.

Bake for 20-25 minutes or until golden and fluffy.

Freezer tip: Once the scones are shaped, chill in the freezer until firm. Transfer to a freezer bag and store up until 3 weeks. When ready to serve, place on a baking tray and follow the recipe instructions above.

STRAWBERRY ALMOND SCONES

MAKES 8

I used fresh strawberries in this recipe because they lend a brightness that pairs well with the warm almond flavor. Raspberries can be easily substituted as well as dried strawberries if you can find them. Deliciously light and flaky, they are the perfect accompaniment to a hot cup of tea.

6 ounces unsalted butter, diced and cold

The Dry Ingredients:
2 cups all-purpose flour, plus more for dusting
1/4 cup granulated sugar
1 tablespoon baking powder
1/2 teaspoon salt
The Wet Ingredients:
1/2 cup heavy whipping cream, cold
½ teaspoon pure almond extract
2 large eggs, cold

The Mix Ins:
1 heaping cup chopped strawberries
(about 1/2 pound)
½ cup sliced almonds

For the glaze:
3/4 cup powdered sugar
1 tablespoon milk
¼ teaspoon almond extract

Preheat the oven to 400 °F, 200 °C.

Place the flour, sugar salt and baking powder in a large bowl and whisk together. Place in a food processor fitted with the blade attachment. Add the butter and pulse until the mixture resembles coarse meal or until pea sized flour coated butter appears.

In another bowl, whisk together the wet ingredients Add them to the food processor and pulse until it all comes together and forms a ball of dough.Turn the dough out onto a lightly floured counter and gently knead in the strawberries and almonds about 4-5 times. Be careful not to overwork the dough. You do not want to melt the butter.

Shape the dough into a circle about 1 inch in thickness.

Slice it into 8 equal triangular pieces. Just like you would slice a pizza and place the scones onto a baking sheet lined with parchment paper.

Chill in the freezer 15 minutes or until firm.

Sprinkle some sugar over top and bake for 18-22 minutes or until golden.

Combine all the glaze ingredients together in a bowl and whisk together until smooth.

Once the scones are done baking, allow them to cool for 10-15 minutes on a cooling rack.

Drizzle with the glaze and serve.

Freezer Tip: same as cinnamon raisin & walnut scones.

CHOCOLATE HAZELNUT SPREAD

MAKES 2 CUPS

This luxurious chocolate spread is even better than the world-famous Nutella brand. It's much easier to make than you think. Just 5 ingredients. 6 if you count the pinch of salt... That's all! It makes a beautiful homemade gift and can be added to anything.

1 cup hazelnuts
12 ounces high quality milk chocolate
2 tablespoons vegetable oil
3 tablespoons confectioner's sugar
1 tablespoon cocoa powder
pinch of salt

Preheat the oven to 350 °F, 180 °C.

Spread the hazelnuts in a single layer on a baking sheet and toast them in the oven for about 10 minutes.

You may also toast them in a skillet over medium heat, turning them often so that they do not burn. This will take about 8 minutes until they are slightly browned, and their skins begin to blister.

Wrap them in a kitchen towel and rub vigorously to remove as much loose skin as possible. (there will still be some skin left on the hazelnuts. It is ok.)

Let cool completely.

Place the hazelnuts with a pinch of salt in a food processor and grind them until they form a paste and become shiny.

The oil will begin to separate. This will take a few minutes so keep going until they are properly ground. This will ensure that you end up with a very smooth spread. The mixture will also begin to heat up. This is perfect to melt the chocolate that will be added next.

Add all the remaining ingredients and blend well until completely smooth.

The hazelnut spread will be runny and warm, but it will continue to thicken as it cools. My favorite time to eat it is a day later.

Store this decadent treat in a jar at room temperature for two weeks. I don't know of any case where it's lasted that long....

DEVONSHIRE CREAM

MAKES 1 AND ½ CUPS

Without a doubt, clotted cream is the perfect accompaniment to scones. Since, it is very hard to find and not so easy to make, I decided to create something very similar using creamy mascarpone cheese. It's delicious!

1 cup mascarpone cream
1/2 cup heavy whipping cream
¼ cup sour cream
1 teaspoon vanilla extract
1 tablespoon confectioner's sugar

Place all the ingredients in a bowl and beat with an electric mixer until the mixture becomes creamy and fluffy.

Keep refrigerated until ready to serve.

This is best made the day that you will be serving it with your scones.

FRUIT FLAVORED BUTTER

SERVES 6

Homemade flavored butter is very simple to make. Spread it on hot bread, pound cake, serve it with scones, French toast, pancakes.... The list is endless as are the flavor combinations that can be created with this basic recipe. Use your favorite jam or pureed preserves to create your desired butter.

Apricot Butter:
4 ounces unsalted butter, softened
¼ cup apricot jam
1/8 teaspoon salt

Orange Butter:
4 ounces unsalted butter, softened
¼ cup orange marmalade
1/8 teaspoon salt

Strawberry Butter:
4 ounces unsalted butter, softened
¼ cup strawberry jam
1/8 teaspoon salt

Cherry Butter:
4 ounces unsalted butter, softened
¼ cup cherry preserves, pureed
¼ teaspoon almond extract
1/8 teaspoon salt

Place the butter in a bowl and beat with an electric mixer until fluffy.

Add the remaining ingredients and beat until incorporated.

Transfer to a serving bowl and store any leftovers in the refrigerator.

SAVORIES

ASPARAGUS TART WITH SMOKED SALMON

SERVES 6

Fresh asparagus combined with a creamy ricotta and feta filling would be delicious all on its own. Add puff pastry and smoked salmon to the list of ingredients and you'll have a tart elegant enough to present at brunch and simple enough to enjoy any busy day of the week.

1 cup (9 ounces) of Ricotta cheese
1 cup (5-6 ounces) crumbled feta (or more, if you're like me)
1 tablespoon whole milk plain yogurt
2 tablespoons of finely chopped or sliced fresh mint
20-25 asparagus spears, woodsy ends trimmed
about 1 cup cherry tomatoes
3 tablespoons olive oil
1/4 -1/2 teaspoon dried oregano
Salt and freshly ground pepper
1 (approx. 14 ounce) sheet Puff Pastry, thawed
4 ounces thinly sliced smoked salmon

Egg wash:
1 egg yolk plus 3-4 tablespoons water or milk, whisked together

Preheat the oven to 400 °F, 200 °C

Combine the ricotta cheese, feta, yogurt, and mint and mix well. Taste and season with desired amount of salt and pepper.

Place the asparagus spears and tomatoes on a tray. Pour olive oil over the vegetables and season with salt and oregano. Add some freshly ground black pepper if desired.

Lightly dust a work surface with some flour. Roll out the puff pastry sheet into a 10 by 16-inch rectangle.

Place the dough on a baking sheet lined with parchment paper.

With a sharp knife, score a line inside the border of the puff pastry 1/2 inch from the edge, marking a rectangle. Do not cut all the way down to the bottom.

Prick the inside rectangle of the pastry with a fork all around. This will prevent the center of the tart from puffing up too much while baking and will allow the border to create a nice puffy crust.

Spread the cheese mixture inside the rectangle keeping it off the borders.

Arrange the marinated asparagus spears over the cheese and top with tomatoes.

Brush the edges of the tart with egg wash.

Bake for about 20-25 minutes or until golden and puffy.

Allow to cool for about 15 minutes before serving. Arrange smoked salmon slices over tart and serve.

HALOUMI & TOMATO TART

SERVES 6

I love serving tarts at brunch. I also love puff pastry. I love cheese. I love pesto and roasted tomatoes. A lot of love in this recipe, so you can bet your (fill in the blank) it will be good! Haloumi cheese is also known as grilling cheese and can be found in your local Mediterranean/Middle Eastern grocery store. It holds its shape and doesn't melt. If you prefer a creamier cheese, go ahead and substitute feta cheese for the Haloumi.

1 (8 ounce) sheet puff pastry, thawed
1/2 cup Pesto Sauce
1-pint cherry or grape tomatoes, halved
1/2-pound halloumi cheese
2 tablespoon olive oil
salt and pepper, to taste
1 teaspoon dried oregano
1/4 cup pine nuts (optional)

Preheat oven to 400 °F, 200 °C.

Lightly dust a work surface with some flour. Roll out the puff pastry sheet into a 10 by 16-inch rectangle.

Place the dough on a baking sheet lined with parchment paper.

With a sharp knife, score a line inside the border of the puff pastry 1/2 inch from the edge, marking a rectangle. Do not cut all the way down to the bottom.

Prick the inside rectangle of the pastry with a fork all around. This will prevent the center of the tart from puffing up too much while baking and will allow the border to create a nice puffy crust.

Place the puff pastry in a half sheet baking tray lined with parchment paper.

Place the sliced tomatoes in a bowl, drizzle with olive oil and season with salt, pepper, and oregano. Toss to coat.

Slice the halloumi cheese into squares double the size of the tomatoes.

Spread the pesto sauce along the inside of the tart.

Create a row of tomatoes.

Layer the halloumi next and continue until the inside of the tart is filled with halloumi and tomato slices.

Sprinkle the pine nuts over the halloumi and tomatoes.

Brush the border of the pastry with the juices from the tomato marinade.

Bake for 20-25 minutes.

Serve warm.

KOTOPITA: GREEK STYLE CHICKEN & PHYLLO PIE

SERVES 12

An explosion of flavors. That is the best way to describe this dish. Roasted chicken, peppers, cheese, all wrapped in buttery, crisp phyllo. Perfect for entertaining since it's served family style in one pan. Serve alongside a nice salad and brunch is served!

For the Roasted Chicken:
1 whole roaster chicken
1/4 cup olive oil
salt and freshly ground black pepper
1/4 cup dried oregano
1 teaspoon cumin powder
pinch of crushed red pepper flakes (optional)

For the Filling:
1/4 cup olive oil
1 large onion, diced
2 garlic cloves, whole
2 bell peppers, diced
1 teaspoon fresh thyme or rosemary
other optional vegetables: chopped carrots, sliced mushrooms
salt and freshly ground pepper
pinch of crushed red pepper flakes
1 cup crumbled feta cheese
1 cup shredded parmesan cheese
1 cup grated gouda or mozzarella cheese

For the Béchamel Sauce:
2 cups whole milk
1/4 cup olive oil
1/4 cup all-purpose flour
salt and freshly ground pepper
1/4 teaspoon ground nutmeg
2 eggs

For the Crust:
1-pound phyllo pastry, thawed and at room temperature
1/2-pound unsalted butter, melted
a few tablespoons of sesame seeds

note: I made this pie many times in various baking pans:
A 10 inch round deep-dish pie pan produces a thicker pie.
A half sheet baking tray (12 by 17 inches) makes a thinner pie like the kind sold in Greece.
A 13 by 9-inch baking pan creates my favorite serving portion. Not too thick and not too thin.
Use whichever pan you have or prefer. You may even bake this in 2 smaller pans.

Preheat the oven to 400 °F, 200 °C.

Wash the chicken with cold water and pat it dry. Pour the olive oil over the chicken and season both sides with the herbs and spices.

Cover the chicken with aluminum foil and bake for 40 minutes.

Remove the foil and bake uncovered 40 additional minutes or until the chicken is fully cooked.

Cool completely.

In the meantime, make the filling by cooking the garlic cloves with the diced onions and oil in a pan for about 15 minutes or until soft.

Add the diced bell peppers, season with some salt and pepper and cook 5-6 minutes or until they soften and release their juices.

When the chicken is cool enough to handle, remove the meat and set the bones aside to make broth another day.

Shred the meat or chop it. About 4 cups are needed for this recipe.

Add the meat and the sautéed pepper mixture to a large bowl and mix well to combine.

Add some fresh thyme and taste to see if any more salt and pepper is needed.
I always add a pinch of crushed red pepper flakes for some heat.

Make the béchamel sauce by combining the olive oil and flour to a saucepan. Cook over medium heat while whisking until it becomes slightly toasted.

Add the milk, salt. pepper, and nutmeg. Whisk well to combine. Take care to not add too much salt. There will be lots of cheese in the filling which is already salty.

Bring the mixture to a boil and continue whisking until it thickens enough to coat the back of a spoon. Remove from heat.

Lightly beat the 2 eggs in a bowl.

Add about a cup of the hot creamy mixture to the eggs. Whisk to incorporate and to raise the temperature of the eggs, so that they don't scramble.

Add the egg mixture to the saucepan and whisk well to combine.

Pour the béchamel sauce into the mixing bowl with the filling. Add the cheeses and mix well.

Remove the phyllo from its packaging. Separate it into 2 equal stacks. One will be for the bottom and the other for the top of the pie. I like to use a little more for the bottom and less for the top. It's a matter of personal preference. The pie will still be delicious either way.

Brush the baking pan with melted butter.Take 2-4 sheets of phyllo and place them at the 12:00 position of the pan (as if you were looking at a clock) placing half (the wide way) in the pan and the other half should hang out of the pan.

Drizzle some melted butter on top of the phyllo.

Take 2-4 more phyllo sheets and place them at the 3:00 position of the baking pan, half in and half hanging out.

Drizzle them with some more melted butter.

Take 2-4 more phyllo sheets and place them down in the bottom of the pan. Drizzle with melted butter.

Take 2-4 phyllo sheets and place them at the 9:00 position of the baking pan. Drizzle with butter.

Pour all the filling onto the pan and cover it with the phyllo that is hanging outside of the pan.

Drizzle with melted butter.

Take 1 stack (2-4 sheets) of phyllo and place on top, tucking the edges in well.

Drizzle with melted butter and continue this process until all the phyllo and butter runs out.

Score the pie into 12 equal pieces and pour the remaining butter all over the pie.

Sprinkle the top with some sesame seeds.

Bake 45 -60 minutes or until the pie is golden brown on top and the filling is bubbling. Sometimes, it can take 1 hour and 15 minutes to be ready.

Allow the pie at least 20-30 minutes to rest at room temperature so that the filling sets and it will be easy to slice and serve.

note: Phyllo pastry comes in various thicknesses. The thinner the phyllo, the more sheets will be in a pack. The thicker phyllo will have fewer sheets since it is sold by weight. I usually buy the #4 thickness. Any phyllo will do.

PHYLLO BEEF TURNOVERS WITH MOZZARELLA CHEESE

MAKES 12

Flaky phyllo brushed with butter and filled with a flavorful meat sauce. These can be made ahead and baked to perfection to serve one or a crowd.

Flaky phyllo brushed with butter and filled with a flavorful meat sauce. These can be made ahead and baked to perfection to serve one or a crowd.

Ingredients

1 recipe Basic Meat Sauce, very thick (recipe follows)

1-pound phyllo pastry, thawed and at room temperature

1/2-pound unsalted butter, melted

7-8 ounces mozzarella cheese cut into chunks or shredded

Preheat the oven to 350 °F, 180 °C.

Cut the phyllo in half while it is still in the plastic packaging.
Keep a lightly damp towel with a dry kitchen towel handy to keep the phyllo covered so that it does not dry out and crumble.

Cover the phyllo first with the dry towel and then with the damp towel.

Layer three strips of phyllo drizzling each layer with some melted butter.

Place a heaping tablespoon of the meat sauce on the bottom and top with a few chunks of mozzarella.

Fold flag style and place on a baking sheet lined with parchment paper. See illustration in spinach pie triangles recipe.

Continue to do this until all of the meat sauce and phyllo is finished. This batch makes about 12 large turnovers. You can also make smaller appetizer sized triangles by cutting the roll of phyllo into 3 equal portions instead of 2.

Brush the top of each turnover with the melted butter.

Bake for 25-30 minutes or until golden and crisp.

These freeze beautifully and are great to have ready to bake.

Freezer Tip: Place the uncooked turnovers onto a baking sheet and wrap with plastic wrap. Store in the freezer up to 1 month.
When ready to bake, preheat oven to 350 °F, 180 °C. Place as many turnovers as you want to serve onto a baking tray lined with parchment paper. Cover with foil. Bake covered for 30 minutes. Remove foil and bake uncovered for an additional 15 minutes or until golden and crisp.

Serve these with a nice soup or salad or as is with a side of Tzatziki Sauce

BASIC MEAT SAUCE RECIPE

1-pound lean ground beef
1/3 cup olive oil
1 onion, finely chopped
4 garlic cloves, peeled
1 (16 ounce) can crushed tomatoes
1 teaspoon dried oregano
salt and pepper to taste
pinch of crushed red pepper flakes
1/4 cup chopped fresh parsley, cilantro or basil
1 cup water

Begin by combining the chopped onion, garlic cloves and olive oil in a medium saucepan.

Cook over medium low heat for about 15 minutes or until soft and golden. At this point the garlic cloves will be very soft. Smash them with a wooden spoon or a spatula. They will melt into the sauce.

Add the ground beef and mix well over high heat.

Add the crushed tomatoes, salt, pepper, red pepper flakes and oregano. Mix to combine.

Pour the cup of water over everything and mix one more time.

Bring to a boil then reduce the heat to medium. Cook for about 15-20 minutes or until the sauce has thickened to the consistency that you prefer. You may cook it longer if you like a more concentrated, thick meat sauce or you can even add a little more water if you like a thinner sauce.

Garnish with fresh chopped parsley and enjoy!

SPANAKOPITA: SPINACH PIE ENTRÉE SIZE

MAKES 12 SERVINGS

A classic and very well-known vegetarian Greek dish. Most recipes require an extra step of cooking the spinach and herbs before putting the pie together. My mom taught me how to make it without that extra step and the result is a fresh tasting, juicy filling with a crisp crust. A definite crowd pleaser that freezes beautifully.

1-pound phyllo pastry, at room temperature
1-pound baby spinach, chopped
2 bunches fresh dill, finely chopped or 3 heaping teaspoons dried dill
about 6 scallions, thinly sliced
15 ounces ricotta cheese, full fat and at room temperature
1-pound feta cheese, crumbled
3 eggs, beaten and at room temperature
about 2 cups olive oil, separated
1/2 teaspoon salt
1 teaspoon ground black pepper, or to taste

Important Tips:

1) I can't stress enough how important it is to properly thaw out the phyllo. The best way to do this is by defrosting it overnight in your refrigerator (since it's usually sold in the freezer section). Take it out in the morning or at least 2 hours before you use it and leave it in its packaging to come to room temperature. Do not take it out of the air tight plastic packaging until you are ready to use it. Exposing phyllo to air causes it to crumble and dry out.

2) Use full fat cheeses. Low fat and fat free varieties are not substitutes.

3) Add the eggs to your mixture last so that you can taste and adjust the seasoning without having to consume raw egg.

4) Baby spinach is very easy to find in America. You can buy regular, fresh spinach that is sold in bunches. Just make sure to wash it very well. Baby spinach is convenient since it is already washed and ready to use. That said, use what you can find.

Preheat oven to 450 °F, 230 °C.

Combine the chopped spinach, dill, scallions, ricotta and feta cheese in a large bowl and using your very clean hands, mix very well.

Knead it, crush it and keep mixing until everything is combined well. This can also be done in a stand mixer fitted with the paddle attachment.

Taste the mixture and add as much salt and pepper as you like.

Add the beaten eggs and about 1 cup of olive oil and mix well.

Grease a half sheet (18-in. x 13-in. x 1-in.) baking pan

Lay 3 sheets on the bottom of pan and drizzle with a little olive oil.

Place 2 sheets half in the pan and half hanging outside of the pan on all four sides of pan.

Spread all of the filling inside of the phyllo sheets. All of the sheets that are hanging outside of the pan should go over the filling to cover.

Drizzle some olive oil all over the phyllo.

Cover half of the pie with 2 sheets of phyllo, tucking them under and repeat the same with the other side of the pie.

Take the remaining phyllo sheets, one at a time, and forming a wrinkled ball, place them in rows on top of the pie.

Drizzle all the remaining olive oil on top of them. This will create a crisp, light crust.

Using a very sharp knife cut the pie into 12 equal slices.

Place in oven and immediately reduce the temperature to 350 °F. Bake for 1 hour. The pie will be crisp and golden brown.

Allow to rest at room temperature for at least 20 minutes before serving. This will allow the filling to set.

SPANAKOPITA TRIANGLES: MINI SPINACH PIE TRIANGLES

MAKES 20-24

Spanakopita has got to be one of the most well-known Greek dishes on the planet. Its light and flaky phyllo crust is delicious and compliments the creamy filling perfectly. I love serving this at brunch, dinner parties, or even when guests just stop by to visit. It's one of those recipes (my favorite kind) that freeze well and go from freezer to oven to table with very little effort.

1 (1 pound) pack phyllo dough, at room temperature
½ pound baby spinach leaves, chopped
1 bunch fresh dill, finely chopped (or 2 teaspoons dried dill)
3 scallions, thinly sliced
8 ounces ricotta cheese, full fat and at room temperature
1/2 pound feta cheese, crumbled
2 eggs, beaten and at room temperature
1 cup olive oil or melted butter
salt and freshly ground black pepper to taste

Important Tips: see spanakopita entree recipe tips

Preheat your oven to 375 °F, 190 °C.

Combine the chopped spinach, dill, scallions, ricotta and feta cheese in a large bowl and using your very clean hands, mix very well. Knead it, crush it and keep mixing until everything is combined well. This can also be done in a table top mixer fitted with the paddle attachment.

Taste the mixture and add as much salt and pepper as you like.

Add the beaten eggs and about 1/2 cup of olive oil and mix well.

Line a baking sheet with parchment paper.

Take the phyllo dough out of its box and cut it into 3 equal pieces (while it's still wrapped in plastic).

Take 2 strips of phyllo at a time and place a tablespoon of filling on the bottom. Fold it up, flag style. See beef turnover illustration.

Sometimes the phyllo sticks together. You don't have to be precise and fight with it to stick to the 2 layers of phyllo rule. 3 layers will work perfectly here.

Keep going until you run out of filling.

Traditionally, oil or melted butter is brushed between each layer and you can do it that way, but I found a shortcut! And who doesn't like shortcuts?

Pour enough olive oil over the prepared spinach pie triangles (about 1/2 cup or more) to coat them and brush it all over with a pastry brush so that they are all coated and some oil seeps in between them. This step saves a lot of time.

Bake them for about 25 minutes or until nice and golden. Serve with tzatziki or as is.

Freezer Instructions: Once the spinach pies are formed and, in the tray, lined with parchment, wrap them air tight with plastic wrap and store in the freezer (up to one month) until ready to bake.

To bake the frozen spinach pies, just take off the plastic wrap and pour and brush olive oil over them just like we did for the freshly made pies. Do not thaw them out!!!

Cover with foil. Tent the foil so that it does not stick on the top layer of phyllo. It's a good idea to brush some oil on the foil as well or to spray some cooking spray to prevent sticking.

Bake covered with foil in a preheated 350 °F oven for about 45 minutes. Remove foil and bake for another 15 minutes or until nice and golden.

PERFECT ROASTED POTATOES

Roasted potatoes are the perfect side to any meal. Serving them at brunch adds that hearty touch with very little effort.

6 medium Russet or Red potatoes, washed and cubed
1/2 cup water
1/4 cup olive oil
1/8 - 1/4 cup freshly squeezed lemon juice
1 teaspoon salt
1 teaspoon oregano
black pepper, to taste
1/4 teaspoon crushed red pepper flakes
finely sliced scallions for garnish (optional: sprigs of rosemary)

Preheat oven to 450 ° 230 °C.

Place chopped potatoes and water on a baking tray.

Drizzle with olive oil and lemon juice.

Sprinkle the salt, peppers, oregano and mix well to coat.

Spread the potatoes on the tray and bake for 25-35 minutes or until crisp on the outside and fully cooked inside.

As soon as the potatoes come out of the oven, sprinkle the scallions over top.

Transfer to a serving platter and serve warm.

SALMON NICOISE SALAD

This beautiful French salad is perfect as a main course at brunch. It's fresh, light, and very easy to prepare. There's no fussing over keeping it hot since it's a salad. Get creative with vegetables that are in season when serving this delicious dish.

FOR THE SALMON:
About 2 pounds salmon filets
Juice of 2 lemons
2 tablespoons olive oil
Salt and freshly ground black pepper to taste
1 teaspoon dried oregano

THE SALAD:
½ pound haricots verts, trimmed (green beans)
6 large eggs
2 pounds baby potatoes (new potatoes or any other small variety)
1 cup olives
10 ounces grape or cherry tomatoes
1 head of lettuce, Bibb lettuce, arugula, or baby greens
Good quality olive oil for drizzling over vegetables
Bowl filled with ice water for the green beans

THE VINAIGRETTE:
½ cup extra virgin olive oil
¼ cup freshly squeezed lemon juice
1 garlic clove, minced
1 teaspoon Dijon mustard, or more
1 teaspoon dried crushed oregano
½ teaspoon salt

Preheat oven to 475 °F, 250 °C.

Combine the juice of 2 lemons, 2 tablespoons olive oil, and oregano in a bowl and whisk well to combine.

Place the salmon fillets on a baking sheet.

Pour the marinade over fish and season both sides with salt and freshly ground black pepper.

Roast for 15 minutes. Set aside to cool completely.

Place potatoes in a pot, cover with water and season with salt.

Bring to a boil and cook until fork tender, about 15 minutes.

Do not strain the water. Instead, take the potatoes out of the hot water using a slotted spoon and set aside to cool.

Bring the pot of water to a boil and add the green beans (haricots verts). Boil about 2 minutes until tender.

Take the beans out of the boiling water with a slotted spoon and immerse immediately in a bowl filled with ice and water.

Place the eggs in the pot with boiling hot water that the vegetables were boiled in. Boil the eggs for 8 minutes.

Remove the green beans from the ice water and place the boiled eggs in the water to cool down.

As soon as the eggs have cooled, peel them and slice in half.

Combine all the vinaigrette ingredients in a bowl and whisk well to combine.

Arrange lettuce leaves on a serving platter and season lightly with salt.

Slice the potatoes in half. Peel or leave as is.

Place the potatoes in a bowl and drizzle some olive oil and ¼ of the vinaigrette over them.

Toss to combine while still warm and season with salt.

Arrange the vegetables over the lettuce in sections on the serving platter, leaving an empty space in the center for the salmon.

Break the salmon into large flakes and place on the platter.

Drizzle the remaining vinaigrette over the vegetables and fish. Add some more olive oil and salt if desired.

Serve cold or at room temperature.

Note: Make an extra batch of ladolemono (lemony olive oil) vinaigrette and serve it in a small pitcher alongside this dish. That way, guests can add more if they desire.

CREAMY ROASTED CAULIFLOWER SOUP

SERVES 8

The first time I ate cauliflower in the form of a soup was at "The Vintage Garden Tea House" up in Montgomery, Texas. It was served in a fancy tea cup topped with a flaky, baked puff pastry circle and it was delicious! So, I was inspired to create my version of it. Roasting vegetables really concentrates their flavor and adds a bit of natural sweetness to them. So, naturally, it's my favorite way to eat veggies. This soup is full of flavor and it freezes well. Perfect for making ahead and having it ready for those busy days.

1 Cauliflower heart, washed and separated into florets
1 medium onion, chopped
½ cup olive oil
4 garlic cloves
1 potato, peeled and chopped
1 carrot, peeled
Chicken stock or water
Heavy cream
Parmesan cheese or kefalotiri
Dried oregano
Crushed red pepper flakes
¼ teaspoon cumin powder
Salt and freshly ground pepper to taste

Preheat your oven to 400 °F, 204 °C.

Chop one head of cauliflower or separate the florets and place on a half sheet baking pan along with one medium chopped onion, 4 whole cloves of garlic, one medium or large chopped potato and the carrot.

Drizzle 1/2 a cup of olive oil over the veggies, and sprinkle with salt and black pepper.

Mix well to incorporate.

Roast the veggies for 35-40 minutes or until tender, turning them halfway through cooking.

Set the carrot aside and chop it into small pieces.

Also set aside four or five cauliflower florets.

Puree all the rest of the vegetables in a few batches with water or chicken stock. This can be done in a few batches using a blender.

Puree until very creamy and pour into a pot.

Add the 4-5 pieces of cauliflower that you reserved with about 2 cups of water or chicken stock and slowly bring to a boil while stirring.

Reduce to a simmer.

Season with salt, a pinch of crushed red pepper flakes, 1/4 teaspoon of cumin powder and 1/2 teaspoon of dried, crushed oregano.

Keep stirring it occasionally so that it does not burn. Let it simmer for about 30 minutes and while stirring, break up the cauliflower florets to add texture to the creamy soup.

Add the chopped roasted carrot with 2 cups of heavy cream. Heat to a simmer while stirring.

Taste the salt and add more if needed.

Pour into bowls and sprinkle some grated parmesan or kefalotiri cheese. Toast some pita or Italian bread and Enjoy!

Optional:
Thaw out a sheet of puff pastry and cut out some circles or squares.

Brush with some egg wash (1 egg yolk mixed with 2 tablespoons water) and season with salt and pepper.

Bake until golden and crisp.

These rounds can be served on top of each bowl or cup.

Make Ahead Freezer Tips:
Make the soup and do not add cream to it. Allow it to cool completely and store in freezer safe bags or containers. Thaw out in the refrigerator one day before serving. Warm through in a pot and add cream. Serve.

Turn into Chicken Pot Pie by pureeing only half of the veggies and chopping the rest into smaller bite sized pieces. Bring to a simmer and add cream along with chopped roasted or rotisserie chicken. Top with puff pastry and bake until golden and crisp.

SMOKED SALMON TEA SANDWICHES

MAKES 16 TRIANGLES

These dainty sandwiches are one of the most popular served at high tea. Use the same cheese filling with thinly sliced cucumbers and a white bread and serve along with some scones, fresh fruit, and little pastries at afternoon tea. I especially love that they can be prepared a day ahead.

4.5 ounces cream cheese, softened at room temperature
1 tablespoon yogurt
1 tablespoon dried dill
1 teaspoon chopped chives
1/4 lemon, zest and juice
8 ounces smoked salmon slices
8 slices of your favorite whole wheat bread

Combine the cream cheese and yogurt in a bowl and mix with a spatula or spoon until fluffy and smooth.

Add the dill, chives, lemon zest and juice and whisk well until incorporated and fluffy.

With a serrated knife, cut the corners of the bread slices (save them to make breadcrumbs)

Spread a layer of the cream cheese filling over each slice of bread.

Place a slice or two of smoked salmon over 4 of the bread slices.

Top with the other slice of bread to create a sandwich.

Slice each sandwich diagonally with a serrated knife to create triangular shaped sandwiches. You will end up with a total of 16 triangles.

Serve immediately or store in the refrigerator up to one day.

To store properly in the refrigerator, place the prepared sandwiches on a tray lined with parchment paper. Cover the sandwiches with a dry paper towel and then on top with a moist paper towel (so that they do not dry out).

Wrap the entire tray with plastic wrap and store in the refrigerator.

This is perfect for a brunch or tea party. You can make plenty of these delicious sandwiches the day before your party.

To make cucumber tea sandwiches:

Use the same spread with the optional addition of finely sliced fresh mint.

Use white sandwich bread instead of dark.

Spread the cheese filling on both sides of bread, Place a layer of cucumber slices on one of the slices of bread.

Top with the other bread slice. Cut into 4 squares and serve.

CREAMY ROASTED TOMATO SOUP WITH GRILLED CHEESE CROISSANT

SERVES 6-8

This tomato soup is full of flavor and pairs beautifully with a Grilled Cheese Croissant. Recipe will be below the soup.

2 pounds Roma (plum) tomatoes, about 16 tomatoes
2 small onions, peeled and quartered
5-6 garlic cloves
1/3 cup olive oil
salt and freshly ground black pepper, to taste
2 tablespoons dried basil
pinch of crushed red pepper flakes
1/4 cup tomato paste
3/4 cup heavy whipping cream
1 quart water or vegetable broth
fresh basil for garnish

Preheat the oven to 450 °F, 230 °C.

Wash and dry the tomatoes. Cut them into 4 pieces each and place in a tray.

Add the quartered onions to the pan.

Drizzle olive oil over the vegetables. Season with salt, pepper, and dried basil. Toss to coat.

Roast for 45 minutes to an hour or until the vegetables at the edges of the pan are caramelized.

Puree the roasted vegetables with the water and tomato paste in 2-3 batches until smooth.

Place the puree in a pot and bring to a boil.

Add some more liquid to thin to your desired consistency.

Season with more salt and pepper if needed.

Stir in the heavy whipping cream.

Garnish with fresh basil or with more dried basil.

Serve hot.

For the Grilled Cheese Croissant:
Makes 1:
1 croissant
1/2 cup shredded mozzarella cheese or gouda
2 tablespoons crumbled feta cheese
1 teaspoon dried basil or oregano

Preheat the oven to 350 °F, 175 °Celsius.

Slice the croissant in half to separate the top and bottom.

Place the cheeses and dried basil on the bottom part of croissant slice. Place the croissant top over the cheese.

Bake the croissant on a tray lined with parchment paper for 5-6 minutes or until the croissant is toasted and cheese is melted

PARMESAN CRISPS

MAKES 6-8

These elegant crisps are the perfect atop salad, for dipping, or just to make things extra special. Make them big or small.

2 cups shredded parmesan cheese
Optional flavorings: dried basil or oregano
Parchment paper

Preheat the oven to 350 °F, 180 °C. Line 2-3 baking sheets with parchment paper.

To make small parmesan crisps, place about 2 tablespoons of shredded parmesan cheese onto the parchment paper and create 3-inch circles.

Be sure to leave space (about 2 inches apart) in between so that they don't join while baking. They will spread.

Bake until golden. About 5 minutes. Keep a close eye on them so that they don't burn. Set aside to cool.

If making the larger parmesan crisps, place about ¼ cup of shredded cheese onto the baking tray lined with parchment and form a 6-inch circle.

Bake until golden. Set aside to cool and harden.

Tip: Mix in your favorite herbs with the cheese (before cooking) if desired. Some crushed red pepper flakes give a nice spicy kick.

PESTO SAUCE

2 cups fresh basil leaves, packed
1 garlic clove
1/2 cup shredded parmesan
1/4 cup chopped walnuts
1/4 cup (or more) olive oil
Sea salt and black pepper, to taste
Some water, if needed to thin out the sauce

Place the garlic clove in the food processor and pulse until finely chopped.

Add the walnuts and pulse until finely ground.

Add the washed basil leaves along with the parmesan cheese and some black pepper and puree until finely ground.

While the food processor is running stream in olive oil until a smooth paste is formed.

You may add a few tablespoons of water if you prefer a thinner sauce.

Add salt to taste.

Store in an airtight container in the refrigerator for up to a week.

TZATZIKI: YOGURT & CUCUMBER DIP

MAKES 2 CUPS

1 English cucumber, peeled
1 and 1/2 cups Greek yogurt
1/2 cup sour cream
1-2 garlic cloves minced
1/2 teaspoon of salt, or to taste
freshly ground black pepper
1 teaspoon chopped dill
olive oil for drizzling
pita bread for dipping

Grate the cucumber and sprinkle with some salt.

Set aside in a bowl to release excess liquid.

In the meantime, combine the yogurt, sour cream, garlic, salt and pepper in another bowl and mix well.

Squeeze the cucumber with your hands or in a clean kitchen towel and discard the liquids that are released.

Add the shredded cucumber to the dip and stir to incorporate.

Mix in the dill.

Drizzle with olive oil and your creamy sauce is ready!

FRUITS

STUFFED STRAWBERRIES OVER A BED OF CHOCOLATE

SERVES 6

One of easiest dessert recipes. Perfect anytime, especially for Mother's Day Brunch!

1 cup of heavy whipping cream, very cold
2-3 tablespoons confectioner's sugar
1 teaspoon vanilla extract
16 strawberries
1 cup chocolate chips
1 tablespoon unsalted butter
1/4 cup heavy whipping cream, or more
splash of vanilla extract

Place chocolate, butter and cream in a heat proof bowl over simmering water.

Do not let the hot water touch the bowl.

Melt the chocolate and then stir in the vanilla extract.

Combine the heavy cream, sugar and vanilla in a bowl. Whip over high speed until it thickens (Greek yogurt consistency).

Transfer the mixture into a pastry bag fitted with a star tip.

Prepare the strawberries by slicing off the green stems.

Place them on a platter (stem side down) and slice an "X" on the pointy tip, cutting almost to the bottom.

Gently spread each strawberry apart and fill with the cream.

Spread the melted chocolate on a plate and place the filled berries on top.

Serve immediately.

Optional flavor variations for filling:
Chocolate Whipped Cream: add 1 teaspoon cocoa powder to cream ingredients and whip together

Almond Cream: add ¼ teaspoon pure almond extract to cream ingredients, whip and fold in some ground, toasted almonds

Devonshire Cream: add ½ cup mascarpone cheese to cream ingredients and whip together

Cheesecake Filling: add ½ cup room temperature cream cheese, plus ¼ teaspoon almond extract to the cream ingredients and whip together

Note: If you prefer a thinner chocolate sauce add some more hot heavy whipping cream until it reaches your preferred consistency.

CANTALOUPE WITH GRAPES & BERRIES

SERVES 4

1 whole ripe cantaloupe
1 bunch purple or black grapes
1-pint raspberries
1 tablespoon granulated sugar
Zest and juice of 1 lemon

Combine the raspberries in a bowl with the sugar, lemon juice, and zest. Mix well to combine and set aside.

Remove cantaloupe skin and seeds. Slice into wedges.

Place the cantaloupe wedges on a serving platter and drape some grapes over each.

Top with the berries and serve.

Note: Feel free to substitute any sweet melon for the cantaloupe. The key is for the fruits to be very ripe and sweet. Smell them at the market. They should smell like the fruit itself.

SUMMER FRUIT SALAD

SERVES 10-12

A great treat to enjoy during the summer when the most delicious fruits are in season. This recipe serves a lot of people so keep that in mind. It stays fresh in the refrigerator the day after you prepare it. It never gets wasted in our home. I love to eat it for breakfast the next day when it's extra cold and all of the flavors have come together.

3 mangoes, peeled and cubed
2 oranges, cut into chunks
1 apple, diced
2 cups grapes, halved
1 pear, diced
3 peaches, diced
4 bananas, peeled and sliced
10 strawberries, sliced
3 cups mango nectar
1/4 - 1/2 teaspoon pink salt
1/4 teaspoon black pepper

Place all fruits in a large bowl.

Pour mango nectar over them.

Season with salt and pepper and mix well.

Refrigerate for at least 3 hours then serve.

Enjoy!

Some great substitutes or additions are: plums, apricots, blueberries, cantaloupe or your favorite summer

BARS

THE PERFECT YOGURT BAR TABLE

Setting up a yogurt bar is a perfect addition to your Brunch menu. Guests can choose what they want and create their own parfaits and you can too! Just set everything on a table and let everyone have fun.

Mason Jars, bowls, or glasses to hold the parfaits
Spoons

The yogurt:
1-2 types of yogurt: Greek or plain whole milk yogurt. Offering Greek yogurt alone would be enough, but some people prefer a thinner, lighter yogurt and plain is great. You can also serve vanilla flavored instead of the plain. Sometimes it's less expensive to buy the plain and just stir in some vanilla extract. Go for the whole milk variety. It's creamier and tastes better than the low-fat varieties.

Fruits:
Bananas
Fresh fruits that are in season such as: berries, melon, peaches... Sweet, ripe fruits are best. Nobody likes sour berries. Sticking to fruits that are in season is usually less expensive. Double plus!
Good quality canned fruit is great. Just look for brands with pure ingredients. The shorter the list, the better. Peaches are my favorite!

Nuts (raw or toasted)
Almonds, walnuts, hazelnuts, pecans. Whatever is easy to find works. Toasting nuts in the oven (325 degrees Fahrenheit) for 5-6 minutes maximizes their flavor. I always buy them raw and toast them myself. Many time the already toasted nuts taste rancid.

Jams, Jellies, Preserves, and nut butters (whatever you like)

Granola (homemade or store-bought)

THE PERFECT OATMEAL BAR

SERVES 8

I love setting up a D.I.Y. oatmeal station at brunch. Guests enjoy customizing their oatmeal bowl and you can join them. Keeping entertaining simple is my motto.

2 cups steel cut oats or rolled oats
6-7 cups of water
1/2 teaspoon salt
1 teaspoon pure vanilla extract

Fresh Fruit Toppings:
Berries, banana slices, chopped apples

Creamers:
Warm milk, warm cream, warm almond milk, warm apple juice

Dried Fruit Toppings:
Raisins, coconut, chopped dried figs, cranberries, chopped dried apricots, dried cherries, dates

Nuts & Seeds toppings:
Toasted almonds, toasted pecans, pumpkin seeds, toasted hazelnuts

Nut Butters:
Chocolate hazelnut spread, peanut butter, almond butter

Sweeteners:
Brown sugar, jams, jellies, preserves, maple syrup, honey

Place the oatmeal, water, and salt in a pot and bring to a boil. Reduce to simmer and cook according to package instructions, depending on which oatmeal you are serving.
The oatmeal can be cooked a day or two before the party and stored in the refrigerator.

Warm through the day of the party adding more water to loosen it up. Transfer to a slow cooker to keep warm during the party. If you do not have a slow cooker, just warm it through right before serving and place in something that retains heat well. An enamel coated cast iron pot works well since it remains warm longer than other pots.

MENUS

BRUNCH MENU FOR THE NOVICE COOK

Sparkling Mango & Orange Refresher

Yogurt Bar

Scrambled Eggs with Spinach and Feta in a Croissant

Tea or Coffee with Palmiers

Honeydew or Cantaloupe Slices with Grapes and berries

The Game Plan

THE DAY BEFORE:

• Clean your home and set the table. Set the yogurt bar by taking out all of the toppings that do not need refrigeration. Place them in their serving bowls and cover tightly with plastic wrap if needed. If serving in jars, cover with the lids. Take out all of the serving spoons, platters, silverware, napkins, glasses, cups, etc. that you will use to serve the food.

• Make the palmiers but do not bake them. Keep them on the baking sheet lined with parchment paper that you will use to bake them, cover with plastic wrap and store either in the freezer or refrigerator. Wherever you have space. If you're running low on space, store them in any airtight container that you have. Just make sure to keep them separate using parchment paper so that they don't stick together.

• Combine the eggs, salt, and pepper in a bowl, beat, and cover with a lid or plastic wrap and store in the refrigerator.

• Refrigerate the juices for the refresher drink. You can juice the oranges today or save it for tomorrow. Just keep it chilled in the refrigerator.

THE MORNING OF THE BRUNCH:

• Wake up 3 hours before your guests arrive and eat something light, drink your tea or coffee and get dressed and ready.

• Slice the croissants and set aside either in a plastic bag or covered with a kitchen towel. I prefer a bag to keep the moisture in.

• Chop the spinach and take out the cheese for the egg sandwiches.

• Slice the melon, set in the serving tray and top with the grapes and berries. Loosely cover with plastic wrap and keep refrigerated.

30 minutes before guests arrive preheat the oven, set the yogurt in the yogurt bar, and finish setting up.

As guests are arriving, or 10 minutes before, place the palmiers in the oven to bake while making the egg and cheese croissant sandwiches.

Serve and have a fabulous time with your guests!

GREEK STYLE BRUNCH MENU

Greek Style Shakshuka

Roasted Potatoes

Greek Coffee or Frappe

Vanilla Flavored Greek Yogurt Parfaits with Walnuts & Honey

Karidopita: Walnut & Honey Cake

The Game Plan

ONE DAY BEFORE:
• Clean your home and set the table. Set the yogurt bar by taking out all of the toppings that do not need refrigeration. Place them in their serving bowls and cover tightly with plastic wrap if needed. If serving in jars, cover with the lids. Take out all of the serving spoons, platters, silverware, napkins, glasses, cups, etc. that you will use to serve the food.

• The Shakshuka will be served with roasted potatoes, but bread should be accompanied to dip I the rich sauce. Either make the bread the day before or buy it.

• Make the walnut and honey cake. Cool and cut into squares or triangles. Store in an air-tight container in the refrigerator.

• Combine the Greek yogurt and vanilla extract in a large bowl and mix well. Fill mason jars or serving cups. Cover and refrigerate.

THE MORNING OF THE BRUNCH:
• Wake up 3 hours before your guests arrive and eat something light, drink your tea or coffee and get dressed and ready.

• Two hours before guests arrive, make the roasted potatoes. Leave them in their tray to reheat right before serving.

One hour before guests arrive, make the Shakshuka sauce.
• Set the walnut cake on a serving tray.

• If serving frappe, set up a station and when guests arrive, assign somebody to be in charge of making the iced coffee for everyone.

• Remove the yogurt jars from the refrigerator, top with the walnuts and drizzle with honey. Place a spoon in each one and set at the table.

Fifteen minutes before guests arrive, simmer the Shakshuka sauce, reheat the potatoes. and place them on a serving tray.
• Toast bread in the oven, slice and set on a cutting board or bread basket.

• As soon as guests arrive, add the eggs to the Shakshuka pan and finish cooking. Garnish with chopped parsley.

If serving Greek coffee, make it for your guests right after food is served and eaten.

Enjoy this delicious brunch!

MAKE AHEAD BRUNCH MENU

It doesn't get easier than this menu. All of the prep work is done before the party! Just a few finishing touches and brunch will be served.

Spinach & Feta Strata

Yogurt Parfaits or Bar

Tea or Coffee with Scones

Chocolate Hazelnut Baklava Rolls

The Game Plan

1-2 WEEKS BEFORE:
• The chocolate baklava rolls can be made up to 2 weeks ahead of time. Make them, place on the same baking sheet lined with parchment paper that they will be baked in. Top with the melted butter. Wrap tightly in plastic wrap and freeze. Do not bake before freezing.

• The scones can also be made, placed in a freezer bag once they have hardened in the freezer and set. Store in the freezer until the day of the party. Do not bake before freezing.

ONE DAY BEFORE:
• Clean your home and set the table. Set the yogurt bar by taking out all of the toppings that do not need refrigeration. Place them in their serving bowls and cover tightly with plastic wrap if needed. If serving in jars, cover with the lids. Take out all of the serving spoons, platters, silverware, napkins, glasses, cups, etc. that you will use to serve the food.

• Prepare the yogurt bar and the tea/coffee station with toppings in their bowls, spoons, sweeteners, etc.....

• Prepare the strata tray in the evening, cover and refrigerate.

THE MORNING OF THE BRUNCH:
• Wake up 3 hours before your guests arrive and eat something light, drink your tea or coffee and get dressed and ready.
One and one-half hour before the guests arrive preheat the oven.

One hour before the guests arrive, place the strata in the oven to bake.
• Slice the scallions or chives and set aside. Sprinkle over strata once it comes out of the oven.

• Thirty minutes before guests arrive, bake the chocolate baklava. Once cooled, place on serving tray.

• Fifteen minutes before guests arrive, prepare the tea or coffee and warm up the cups. Add the yogurt to the yogurt bar.

• As soon as guests arrive, bake the scones.

Enjoy a laid back and delicious brunch with your guests!

MOTHER'S DAY BRUNCH MENU

As a very busy mom of five, I can tell you that as much as I appreciate thoughtful gifts, what I love most is spending quality time with my family. A great gesture would be to prepare a nice brunch that can be enjoyed as a family. Serve your mom tea or coffee in bed with a nice pastry/cake and while she's enjoying it, you can go ahead and prepare this delicious menu.

Hot Tea or Coffee in Bed
Served with Blueberry & Lemon Not Just for Coffee Cake

Sparkling Pink Grapefruit Refresher

Asparagus & Smoked Salmon Tart

Stuffed Strawberries Over a Bed of Chocolate

The Game Plan

ONE DAY BEFORE:
• In every other game plan, cleaning the house the day before is listed at the first task to complete the day before. Moms love a clean home, so it would be a very nice gesture if the family got together and tidied up.

• Make the blueberry cake, allow to cool completely, cover and refrigerate.

• Refrigerate the grapefruit, sparkling water, and limes that will be used to make the refresher.

THE MORNING OF THE BRUNCH:
• Wake up 1-2 hours before mom usually gets up and preheat the oven.

• Make the stuffed strawberry dessert and set aside.

• Make the asparagus tart and bake.

• Warm the blueberry cake in the oven just until warmed through.

• Prepare tea or coffee and serve it along with the blueberry cake in bed to mom.

• While she is enjoying her morning treat, clean the kitchen, set the table, and make the refresher.

Serve the meal and enjoy quality time together!

TEA ROOM STYLE BRUNCH MENU

Many times, guests will offer their help by bringing a dish to take some of the cooking load off of the host. I prefer to ask them to just bring flowers. Nothing fancy. I like to choose 1 type of flower that is easy to find and ask each guest to bring 1 or 2 stems each to complete the tea room theme. That way I don't have to worry about decorations.

2 Types of Tea: Black Tea & Herbal Tea

Strawberry & Almond Scones (or Apricot Almond Scones) Served with Devonshire Cream & Preserves

Smoked Salmon Tea Sandwiches

Cucumber Tea Sandwiches

Spanakopita (Spinach Pie) Triangles

Shortbread Tea Bag Shaped Cookies Dipped in Chocolate

Assorted Fruit: Berries and Grapes

The Game Plan

1 WEEK – 10 DAYS BEFORE:
- The scones can be made up to 2 weeks before the party. I prefer to make them 1 week ahead of time to prevent any freezer smell from getting into them. Do not bake before freezing. Store in an airtight freezer container.
- The spanakopita can also be made 2 weeks ahead of time. Make the triangles, place them on a baking sheet lined with parchment paper (the same tray they will be baked in) wrap tightly a few times with plastic wrap and freeze. Do not bake before freezing.

ONE DAY BEFORE:
- Clean your home and set the table. Set the yogurt bar by taking out all of the toppings that do not need refrigeration. Place them in their serving bowls and cover tightly with plastic wrap if needed. If serving in jars, cover with the lids. Take out all of the serving spoons, platters, silverware, napkins, glasses, cups, etc. that you will use to serve the food.
- Make both kinds of tea sandwiches. Place in a single layer on baking sheets lined with parchment paper. Cover the sandwiches with damp paper towels and wrap tightly with plastic wrap. This will ensure that they are moist the day you will serve them. Store in the refrigerator.
- Make the shortbread cookies. Bake them and store in airtight container. This can be done up to 2 days before.

THE MORNING OF THE BRUNCH:
- Wake up 3 hours before your guests arrive and eat something light, drink your tea or coffee and get dressed and ready.
- Dip the shortbread cookies in chocolate, allow to set, and place in serving dish.
- Mke the Devonshire cream and keep refrigerated until serving.
- Arrange the fruits on the serving platters/tier stands. The fruit is used as something refreshing and to add beauty. Think of these as accents on your serving tray. Traditionally, at high tea, everything is served on 3 tiered trays. If you have these, that's great. Use them. If not, ask around because a friend or family may have some that they can let you borrow. Antique shops usually will have 1 or two beautiful pieces at very affordable prices. If you cannot get hold of one, do not fuss too much over it. Serve the food on what you already own.
- Next, preheat the oven.
- 1 hour before the guests arrive, bake the spanakopita. Allow to cool and arrange on serving plates/tiers/platter.
- ½ hour before the guests arrive, arrange the tea sandwiches on their serving platters.
- Keep water simmering for the tea. Place hot water in the tea cups and tea pots if using to warm them just a few minutes before guests arrive.
- Place the scones in the oven as soon as guests arrive. Set them out with the tea.

Enjoy a delicious brunch with your guests!

THE ELEGANT BRUNCH MENU

This menu is for the more experienced cook. None of these recipes are difficult to make, especially if you follow the recipes closely. Much of the prep work can be done ahead of time and the end result is a very elegant menu that is quite hearty.

Soup Served with Feta & Dill Scones (choose from cauliflower or tomato soup, both recipes are in this book)

Salmon Nicoise Salad

Hazelnut Pavlova with Chocolate Hazelnut Whipped Cream & Raspberries

Tea or Coffee

The Game Plan

ONE WEEK BEFORE:
• Make the scones and freeze them. Do not bake before freezing. Store in airtight freezer container/bag.

TWO DAYS BEFORE:
• Make the soup two days before and refrigerate in the same pot. Do not add cream until the brunch party.

ONE DAY BEFORE:
• Clean your home and set the table. Set the yogurt bar by taking out all of the toppings that do not need refrigeration. Place them in their serving bowls and cover tightly with plastic wrap if needed. If serving in jars, cover with the lids. Take out all of the serving spoons, platters, silverware, napkins, glasses, cups, etc. that you will use to serve the food.

•Make the hazelnut meringue for the Pavlova. Wrap in plastic and store at room temperature.

THE MORNING OF THE BRUNCH
• Wake up 3 hours before your guests arrive and eat something light, drink your tea or coffee and get dressed and ready.

• Preheat the oven.

• Two hours before guests arrive prepare the Salmon salad.

• Warm up the soup on a very low simmer, stirring every few minutes.

• One hour before guests arrive, finish making the Pavlova, put it on a serving tray and keep refrigerated until guests arrive.

• Keep the oven preheated for the scones and bake them thirty minutes before guests arrive.

• Add cream to the soup and check the seasoning.

• Prepare the coffee or tea.

• Set the soup on the serving table alongside the feta scones.

• Right before the guests arrive, set the pavlova on the table as the centerpiece.

Enjoy!

ABOUT DIMITRA

I grew up in a traditional Greek family in New York. All of our meals were homemade, every happy gathering took place around a table full of delicious food that was shared with loved ones. My summers spent visiting family on the beautiful island of Crete are filled with memories of getting together with grandparents, cousins, aunts, and uncles in a laid back happy setting, again, sharing homemade food while creating memories and traditions that now I get to pass down to my own children.

These experiences filled my heart with a deep love of cooking and appreciation of sharing meals with friends and family. The more the merrier! All while keeping it simple and laid back.

I love cooking so much, that I even cooked on my honeymoon! Yes, you read that correctly, after eating out for a few nights, I wanted to make a nice meal for the two of us. I mean, is there any better way to celebrate our new life together? So, I prepared a nice broiled salmon filet with a side of rice pilaf and some salad. The rest is history...

In 2008, right smack dab in the middle of a recession, my husband and I, without any experience in the food business, opened our very first restaurant, Euro Bakery & Café. Just a few years after opening, our guests requested cooking classes, which led to my YouTube video tutorials on Dimitra's Dishes, then the creation of my website where all the written recipes live, and finally, the beginning of writing cookbooks. The best part about this dream come true is all of the emails and messages that I receive from my viewers. I love reading them and hearing your sweet stories and uplifting comments.

Welcome to my journey! Together, we will cook, share, and create memories and make this world a better place. My recipes are always delicious, and worth sharing, very simple to follow and filled with tips from over 10 years of experience in the world of food. I hope these recipes will help you create the most beautiful memories!

Made in the USA
Middletown, DE
12 May 2021